eSport Business

The Rise of Gaming Empires

Ghazwan Alemara

Published by ghazwanalemara.com

Contents

Contents 3

Introduction 1

Chapter 1: Building the Empire: eSports Organizations............3

    The Origins of Competitive Gaming 3

    Formation of Professional Teams 10

    The Role of eSports Organizations 14

    Case Study: Success Stories 20

Chapter 2: The Business of eSports 26

    Revenue Models in eSports 26

    Sponsorship and Advertising 31

    Monetizing Content 37

Chapter 3: Technology and Innovation 43

    The Evolution of Gaming Hardware 43

    Streaming Platforms and Their Impact 49

    Emerging Technologies 55

Chapter 4: The Economics of eSports 62

    Market Size and Growth Trends 62

    Investment in eSports 69

    Economic Challenges and Opportunities 75

Chapter 5: The Cultural Phenomenon 81

    The Rise of eSports Fandom 81

    eSports and Mainstream Media 86

    Global Impact and Diversity 91

Chapter 6: Legal and Ethical Landscape 97

Regulation and Governance 97

Player Rights and Contracts 102

Ethical Issues in eSports 107

Chapter 7: The Future of eSports 113

Trends Shaping the Future 113

Potential Challenges 119

Predictions and Opportunities 125

Conclusion 131

Introduction

Welcome to the exhilarating world of eSports, where competitive gaming has evolved into a global phenomenon, captivating millions of fans and generating billions of dollars in revenue. This book is your comprehensive guide to understanding the intricacies of this dynamic industry.

eSports, once a niche hobby enjoyed in arcades and basements, has transformed into a mainstream entertainment powerhouse. From packed stadiums to millions of online viewers, eSports has broken through traditional barriers, drawing in audiences from all walks of life. But beyond the thrilling matches and charismatic players lies a complex and rapidly growing business landscape.

In these pages, we will explore the various elements that make up the eSports ecosystem. You'll discover how organizations are built and managed, the innovative revenue models driving profitability, and the technological advancements that are constantly reshaping the playing field. We'll delve into the critical issues of player welfare, regulatory challenges, and the ethical considerations that are crucial for maintaining the integrity of the sport.

As we start on this journey, it's important to recognize that eSports is more than just a business; it's a cultural phenomenon.

It has fostered communities, built bridges across different cultures, and provided a platform for countless individuals to showcase their talents and passions. Whether you're a budding entrepreneur, a dedicated fan, or someone new to the world of eSports, this book will equip you with the knowledge and inspiration to engage with this vibrant industry.

So, buckle up and get ready to dive into the exciting and ever-evolving world of eSports. From its humble beginnings to its meteoric rise, we'll uncover the factors that have propelled eSports to the forefront of global entertainment.

Chapter 1: Building the Empire: eSports Organizations

The Origins of Competitive Gaming

The story of competitive gaming, or eSports, begins long before the term "eSports" was even coined. The origins can be traced back to the early days of video gaming when arcade machines and home consoles were first introduced. These early platforms laid the groundwork for what would eventually become a global phenomenon.

The First Videogame Tournaments, 1981: The Origin of "eSports".
Source: ma-no.org

Early Arcade Competitions

In the late 1970s and early 1980s, arcades were the epicenters of gaming culture. Players flocked to these vibrant, noisy venues to try their hand at the latest games, challenging themselves and others to achieve high scores. It was in these arcades that the seeds of competitive gaming were first sown. Games like "Space Invaders" and "Pac-Man" became wildly popular, and it wasn't long before informal competitions started to emerge.

One of the earliest recorded competitive gaming events took place in 1980, organized by Atari. The "Space Invaders Championship" attracted more than 10,000 participants across the United States. This event was a significant milestone, highlighting the potential for organized competitive gaming. Players who had previously been isolated in their local arcades now had a platform to compete on a larger scale, and this concept quickly caught on.

The Birth of LAN Parties

As technology advanced, so did the ways in which people played games. The 1990s saw the rise of local area network (LAN) parties, where gamers would bring their own computers to a central location and connect them via a network. This allowed for real-time, multiplayer gaming in a social setting, fostering a sense of community and competition.

One of the most iconic games of this era was "Doom," released in 1993. "Doom" was one of the first games to support multiplayer gameplay over a LAN, and it quickly became a staple at LAN parties. Gamers would spend hours battling each other in the game's dark, labyrinthine levels, and these sessions often turned into impromptu tournaments.

Another landmark game was "Quake," released in 1996. "Quake" took the LAN party scene by storm with its fast-paced, first-person shooter gameplay. It also introduced the concept of the "modding" community, where players could create and share their own modifications to the game. This further fueled the competitive spirit, as players not only competed in the base game but also in custom game modes and maps.

2000s LAN Gaming Party. Source: reddit.com

The Rise of Organized Tournaments

As competitive gaming continued to grow in popularity, it began to attract the attention of larger audiences and organizations.

The late 1990s and early 2000s saw the emergence of organized tournaments, often with significant prize money at stake. These events were pivotal in transforming competitive gaming from a hobby into a professional sport.

One of the first major tournaments was the "Cyberathlete Professional League" (CPL), founded in 1997. The CPL hosted tournaments for games like "Quake" and later "Counter-Strike," offering substantial cash prizes and attracting top talent from around the world. These tournaments were groundbreaking, demonstrating that competitive gaming could be a viable career path.

Another key development was the establishment of the "Electronic Sports World Cup" (ESWC) in 2003. The ESWC brought together the best players from various countries to compete in a range of games, from first-person shooters to real-time strategy games. This international competition helped to legitimize eSports and showcased the diversity and skill of players globally.

The Influence of South Korea

While competitive gaming was gaining traction in the West, it was in South Korea that eSports truly exploded. The late 1990s and early 2000s saw the rise of "StarCraft," a real-time strategy game that became a national obsession. South Korean players dominated the global "StarCraft" scene, and the game's popularity led to the creation of professional leagues and televised matches.

In 2000, the Korean e-Sports Association (KeSPA) was established to oversee and promote the growth of eSports in the country. KeSPA's efforts helped to formalize the industry, providing structure and support for players and teams. This professionalization set a precedent that would be followed by other countries in the years to come.

The impact of South Korea on the eSports landscape cannot be overstated. The country's dedication to competitive gaming helped to elevate it to the status of a legitimate sport, complete with professional players, dedicated fans, and major sponsorships. South Korea's model of professional eSports leagues and televised matches became a blueprint for the global industry.

An eSports Hall of Fame in Seoul's S-plex Center in South Korea.
Source: hapskorea.com

Transition to Global Phenomenon

The 2000s and 2010s saw the transition of competitive gaming from a niche pastime to a global phenomenon. The rise of high-speed internet and streaming platforms like Twitch allowed players and fans to connect and share their passion for gaming like never before. Major tournaments like "The International" for "Dota 2" and the "League of Legends World Championship" drew millions of viewers and offered multi-million-dollar prize pools.

As competitive gaming continued to grow, it attracted significant investment from traditional sports organizations, media companies, and sponsors. Professional teams and players became celebrities in their own right, and the eSports industry evolved into a multi-billion-dollar enterprise.

The origins of competitive gaming are a testament to the passion and dedication of the gaming community. From the early days of arcade competitions and LAN parties to the rise of organized tournaments and professional leagues, the journey of eSports has been nothing short of remarkable. Today, eSports stands as a vibrant and dynamic industry, with a future that looks brighter than ever.

Formation of Professional Teams

The formation of professional eSports teams marked a significant turning point in the evolution of competitive gaming. It transformed the landscape from casual play and amateur tournaments to a structured, organized, and highly competitive arena. Let's explore how these teams were formed, their impact on the industry, and the factors that contributed to their success.

The Early Beginnings

In the late 1990s and early 2000s, as eSports started gaining traction, talented gamers began to realize the potential benefits of forming teams. These early teams were often groups of friends or players who had met through online forums and gaming communities. The primary motivation was simple: to compete at a higher level and achieve greater success in tournaments.

One of the earliest examples of a professional team was Clan 9, formed in 1997 to compete in the game "Quake." Their success inspired other players to form their own teams, and soon, the idea of professional gaming teams began to take hold.

The Role of Sponsorships

As the competitive gaming scene grew, so did the interest from sponsors. Companies began to see the marketing potential of eSports and started investing in teams. These sponsorships provided the financial support necessary for teams to train full-time, travel to international tournaments, and compete at the highest levels.

The influx of sponsorship money led to the formation of more professional teams, each with its own roster of talented players, coaches, and support staff. Sponsors not only provided financial backing but also helped elevate the visibility of eSports, attracting more fans and media attention.

Establishing Team Brands

Professional eSports teams quickly realized the importance of branding. Just like traditional sports teams, they needed to create a strong identity to attract fans and sponsors. Teams adopted unique names, logos, and colors, and they actively engaged with their communities through social media and content creation.

Teams like Fnatic, Team Liquid, and Cloud9 became household names in the eSports world, each with a distinct brand and a loyal fan base. These brands were built not only on competitive success but also on a strong presence in the gaming community.

The Impact of Leagues and Tournaments

The establishment of organized leagues and tournaments played a crucial role in the formation and success of professional eSports teams. Leagues like Major League Gaming (MLG), the Electronic Sports League (ESL), and later, the Overwatch League and League of Legends Championship Series (LCS), provided a structured environment for teams to compete regularly.

These leagues offered stability and consistent opportunities for competition, which helped teams plan their training and development more effectively. Regular competition also meant more exposure and better chances for teams to attract sponsors and build their brands.

The Importance of Team Dynamics

Success in eSports isn't just about individual skill; it's also about how well players work together as a team. The best professional teams invest heavily in building strong team dynamics. This includes not only in-game strategies and communication but also fostering a positive team culture and addressing any interpersonal conflicts that arise.

Coaches and support staff play a vital role in this aspect, helping to develop strategies, analyze opponents, and ensure that players are in the best possible mental and physical condition to perform.

Challenges and Evolution

The journey to forming successful professional eSports teams has not been without its challenges. Teams have had to navigate issues such as player contracts, salary negotiations, and the pressures of maintaining peak performance. Additionally, the rapid growth of the industry has meant that teams must continually adapt to new games, changing tournament formats, and evolving audience expectations.

Despite these challenges, the formation of professional teams has been a cornerstone of the eSports industry's growth. These teams have pushed the boundaries of what is possible in competitive gaming, setting new standards for excellence and professionalism.

Today, professional eSports teams are at the heart of the industry, driving its growth and inspiring the next generation of gamers. Their formation and success story is a testament to the passion, dedication, and innovation that defines the world of eSports.

The Role of eSports Organizations

eSports organizations play a crucial role in the structure and growth of the competitive gaming industry. These entities are responsible for managing teams, organizing tournaments, securing sponsorships, and fostering the development of the eSports ecosystem. Their efforts have transformed eSports from a casual pastime into a professional and lucrative career path for many players.

Formation and Management of Teams

One of the primary roles of eSports organizations is the formation and management of professional teams. These organizations scout for talented players, often holding tryouts and recruiting from amateur leagues or streaming platforms. Once a team is formed, the organization provides the necessary resources for the players to train and compete at the highest levels.

This support includes providing gaming equipment, coaching staff, and facilities for practice. Just like in traditional sports, players need rigorous training and strategic guidance to excel. Coaches and analysts work with the team to develop strategies, review past performances, and prepare for upcoming competitions. This professional approach ensures that teams are well-prepared and competitive.

Securing Sponsorships and Funding

Sponsorships are a vital source of revenue for eSports organizations. They secure deals with various brands that want to reach the gaming audience, which is typically young, tech-savvy, and engaged. Sponsors range from gaming hardware companies to energy drink brands, each seeing the value in associating with popular eSports teams and events.

The funds from sponsorships are used to cover operational costs, pay player salaries, and invest in marketing and promotional activities. Sponsorship deals often include branding on team jerseys, promotional content featuring players, and branded segments during live streams and tournaments. This symbiotic relationship benefits both the sponsors and the eSports organizations, providing financial stability and increased visibility.

Organizing and Participating in Tournaments

eSports organizations are heavily involved in the organization of tournaments and leagues. Some organizations run their own tournaments, providing a platform for both their teams and others to compete. These tournaments range from small, local events to major international competitions with substantial prize pools.

Participation in tournaments is critical for the success and reputation of an eSports organization. Winning or performing well in high-profile tournaments not only brings in prize money but also attracts more fans, sponsors, and media attention. Consistent success in tournaments can elevate an organization's status in the eSports community, leading to further opportunities and growth.

Player Development and Welfare

Beyond just the competitive aspect, eSports organizations are responsible for the overall development and welfare of their players. This includes providing mental health support, physical training, and career development programs. The intense nature of competitive gaming can lead to stress and burnout, so organizations often employ psychologists and wellness coaches to support their players.

Physical health is also important. While eSports might not be physically demanding in the same way traditional sports are, maintaining good physical condition can improve reaction times and endurance. Organizations often provide access to fitness trainers and encourage regular physical activity to keep players in peak condition.

Career development is another crucial area. Many players' careers in eSports are relatively short due to the demanding nature of the industry. Organizations help players plan for their future by offering opportunities in coaching, management, content creation, or other roles within the eSports ecosystem once their competitive careers are over.

Building a Brand and Fanbase

Branding is essential for the growth and sustainability of eSports organizations. A strong brand attracts fans, sponsors, and talented players. Organizations invest in creating a unique identity through logos, merchandise, and engaging content. Social media plays a significant role in this, with organizations actively engaging with fans through platforms like X (Twitter), Instagram, and YouTube.

Content creation is a big part of building a fanbase. Organizations produce a variety of content, including behind-the-scenes videos, player interviews, and live streams. This content helps fans feel connected to the team and its players, fostering loyalty and engagement. The more engaged the fanbase, the more valuable the organization becomes to sponsors and investors.

Community Engagement and Development

eSports organizations also play a vital role in community engagement and development. They often organize grassroots tournaments, fan meet-and-greet events, and educational programs about gaming and eSports. By investing in the community, these organizations help to grow the next generation of players and fans.

These activities also help to demystify eSports and promote its positive aspects. Engaging with schools and youth programs can inspire young gamers and provide them with pathways to pursue a career in eSports. Community involvement ensures that the growth of eSports is sustainable and inclusive.

The Global Impact

The impact of eSports organizations is not confined to one region; it's a global phenomenon. Successful organizations have fanbases around the world, and their influence extends across different cultures and markets. This global reach has helped eSports transcend traditional boundaries, making it one of the most inclusive and diverse entertainment forms.

Through international tournaments and online platforms, eSports organizations bring together players and fans from different countries, fostering a sense of global community. This international presence also opens up new markets for sponsorships and partnerships, further driving the growth of the industry.

eSports organizations are the backbone of the competitive gaming industry. They manage teams, secure sponsorships, organize tournaments, and engage with the community. Their efforts have turned eSports into a professional and global phenomenon, providing opportunities for players and entertainment for millions of fans. As the industry continues to grow, the role of these organizations will only become more significant, shaping the future of eSports.

Case Study: Success Stories

The success of professional eSports teams is a testament to the growth and potential of the industry. Let's delve into the stories of a few standout teams that have not only dominated their respective games but also helped shape the landscape of eSports as we know it.

Team Liquid: A Legacy of Excellence

Team Liquid, founded in 2000, is one of the most storied and successful organizations in eSports history. Initially starting as a "StarCraft II" team, they have since expanded into numerous other games, including "Dota 2," "League of Legends," "CS," and more.

What sets Team Liquid apart is their consistent performance and adaptability. They have won multiple championships across various games, showcasing their ability to recruit top talent and maintain high standards. For instance, their "Dota 2" team won The International 2017, one of the most prestigious tournaments in the eSports world, with a prize pool of over $24 million.

Their success can be attributed to a strong organizational structure, excellent coaching staff, and a commitment to fostering a positive team culture. Team Liquid's management invests heavily in player development, ensuring that athletes are not only skilled but also well-supported in terms of mental and physical health.

Fnatic: Pioneers of Global Domination

Fnatic, founded in 2004, is another eSports giant with a legacy of success. Based in London, Fnatic has made a name for itself in games like "League of Legends," "CS," and "Dota 2." Their "League of Legends" team, in particular, has been a dominant force in the European scene.

One of Fnatic's most notable achievements came in 2011 when their "League of Legends" team won the first-ever League of Legends World Championship. This victory catapulted them into the spotlight and solidified their reputation as a top-tier eSports organization.

Fnatic's approach to success involves a keen eye for talent and a robust training regimen. They have built state-of-the-art training facilities and employ a team of experts, including psychologists, nutritionists, and fitness trainers, to ensure their players are in peak condition. Their focus on holistic player development has been a key factor in their sustained success.

Cloud9: Innovators and Champions

Cloud9, founded in 2013, quickly rose to prominence in the eSports world with their innovative strategies and consistent performances. They have fielded competitive teams in games like "League of Legends," "CS," "Overwatch," and "Fortnite."

One of Cloud9's most significant achievements was winning the ELEAGUE Major: Boston 2018 in "CS."

This victory was historic as it marked the first time an American team won a CS

Major, demonstrating Cloud9's ability to compete at the highest level against the best teams in the world.

Cloud9's success is driven by their willingness to innovate and adapt. They are known for their strategic gameplay and for being early adopters of new training techniques and technologies. Cloud9 also places a strong emphasis on community engagement, using their platform to connect with fans and build a loyal following.

T1: South Korea's Pride

T1, previously known as SK Telecom T1, is synonymous with success in "League of Legends." Founded in 2003, T1 has become one of the most decorated teams in eSports history. Their "League of Legends" team, led by legendary player Lee "Faker" Sang-hyeok, has won multiple World Championships, including in 2013, 2015, and 2016.

T1's dominance can be attributed to their rigorous training programs and strategic genius. They have set the standard for excellence in "League of Legends," with a disciplined approach to practice and a focus on continuous improvement. T1's management has also been adept at scouting and nurturing talent, ensuring a steady pipeline of skilled players.

OG: The Cinderella Story

OG's story is one of perseverance and triumph. Founded in 2015, OG is best known for their incredible success in "Dota 2." Despite being underdogs, OG won The International 2018 and 2019, making history as the first team to win the tournament twice.

Their journey to the top was marked by teamwork, resilience, and a deep understanding of the game. OG's players have shown an uncanny ability to remain calm under pressure and execute their strategies flawlessly, even in the most challenging situations.

OG's success highlights the importance of team synergy and mental fortitude. They have inspired countless fans and aspiring players with their remarkable story of turning adversity into triumph.

These success stories exemplify the diverse paths to greatness in the eSports world. Each team has its unique approach, but common themes of talent, innovation, and a strong support system run through their narratives. As the eSports industry continues to grow, these teams will undoubtedly remain at the forefront, inspiring the next generation of champions.

Chapter 2: The Business of eSports

Revenue Models in eSports

The financial success of eSports hinges on various revenue models that support the industry. These models ensure the sustainability and growth of eSports organizations, players, and tournaments. Understanding these revenue streams is crucial for grasping how eSports has evolved into a multi-billion-dollar industry.

Sponsorships and Advertising

Sponsorships and advertising form the backbone of eSports revenue. Brands recognize the value of the eSports audience, which is primarily composed of young, tech-savvy individuals. Companies ranging from tech giants like Intel and NVIDIA to non-endemic brands like Coca-Cola and Red Bull invest heavily in eSports.

Sponsorship deals can include everything from branded team jerseys and equipment to sponsored segments during live streams. Advertising comes in various forms, including in-game ads, banners on streaming platforms, and sponsored content. These sponsorships not only provide financial support but also enhance the visibility and prestige of eSports teams and events.

Media Rights

Media rights have become a significant revenue source for eSports, similar to traditional sports. Broadcasting tournaments on platforms like Twitch, YouTube, and even traditional TV channels allows organizations to monetize viewership. Major eSports events attract millions of viewers, making media rights highly valuable.

Companies pay substantial fees to secure the rights to broadcast these events, and in return, they generate revenue through advertisements and subscriptions. The increasing interest in eSports from mainstream media has further boosted the value of media rights deals.

Merchandise Sales

Merchandise sales are another important revenue stream for eSports organizations. Fans love to show their support by purchasing branded apparel, accessories, and collectibles. From team jerseys and hoodies to mouse pads and gaming peripherals, merchandise offers fans a way to feel connected to their favorite teams and players.

Limited edition items and collaborations with popular brands often drive significant sales. Online stores, physical pop-up shops at events, and partnerships with major retailers help distribute these products widely, enhancing both revenue and brand recognition.

Ticket Sales and Live Events

Live events, such as tournaments and fan conventions, generate revenue through ticket sales. These events are a cornerstone of the eSports experience, offering fans the opportunity to watch their favorite teams compete in person. The excitement and atmosphere of live eSports events are unparalleled, drawing large crowds.

In addition to ticket sales, these events often feature vendor booths, exclusive merchandise, and meet-and-greet opportunities with players, all of which contribute to the overall revenue. The success of these events demonstrates the strong community aspect of eSports and its ability to draw significant in-person audiences.

Streaming and Content Creation

Streaming and content creation have become lucrative revenue streams for individual players and organizations. Platforms like Twitch and YouTube allow players to broadcast their gameplay, interact with fans, and monetize their content through ads, subscriptions, and donations.

Popular streamers and content creators can earn substantial incomes, especially when they partner with platforms or receive sponsorship deals. This model not only provides financial support but also helps build personal brands and expand the reach of eSports beyond traditional tournament settings.

Prize Money

Prize money from tournaments is a direct revenue source for professional players and teams. Major eSports events offer substantial prize pools, sometimes reaching millions of dollars. This prize money incentivizes players to compete at the highest level and provides a significant financial reward for their efforts.

While prize money can be a substantial income source, it is often supplemented by other revenue streams to ensure financial stability for players and teams. The distribution of prize money also varies, with top teams and players receiving the lion's share, while lower-ranking participants earn less.

In-Game Purchases and Microtransactions

Game developers generate revenue through in-game purchases and microtransactions. These include cosmetic items, skins, and other virtual goods that enhance the gaming experience without affecting gameplay balance. Popular games like "Fortnite," "League of Legends," and "Overwatch" have successfully implemented this model, generating significant revenue.

These purchases are often tied to events, seasons, or special promotions, encouraging players to spend on exclusive items. The continuous release of new content keeps the game fresh and engaging, driving ongoing revenue.

Esports Betting

Esports betting is an emerging revenue stream, mirroring the betting industry in traditional sports. Fans can place bets on the outcomes of matches and tournaments through various online platforms. While this area is still developing and faces regulatory challenges, it has the potential to become a significant revenue source.

Betting adds another layer of engagement for fans, increasing viewership and interest in matches. As regulations evolve and the market matures, eSports betting could contribute substantially to the industry's financial ecosystem.

The diverse revenue models in eSports ensure its continued growth and sustainability. From sponsorships and media rights to merchandise sales and live events, these streams collectively support the industry's infrastructure. As eSports continues to evolve, new revenue opportunities will emerge, further solidifying its place in the global entertainment landscape.

Sponsorship and Advertising

Sponsorship and advertising have become integral to the financial of eSports, propelling the industry from niche competitions to mainstream recognition. This section explores how sponsorships and advertising deals work within eSports, their impact on the growth of the industry, and the key players involved.

The Rise of Sponsorship in eSports

The early days of eSports saw players and teams operating on shoestring budgets, often self-funding their participation in tournaments. However, as the popularity of competitive gaming grew, companies began to recognize the marketing potential of this new and dynamic audience. Sponsorship deals started to emerge, providing much-needed financial support to players and teams.

Major brands quickly saw the opportunity to reach a young, tech-savvy audience that traditional sports could not always capture. Energy drink companies like Red Bull and Monster were among the first to invest in eSports, sponsoring events and individual players. These partnerships helped validate eSports as a legitimate competitive activity and brought substantial financial support to the scene.

Apparel Brands in Esports and Live Streaming. Source: escharts.com

How Sponsorship Deals Work

Sponsorship deals in eSports function similarly to those in traditional sports. Companies provide financial support, products, or services in exchange for brand visibility and marketing opportunities. This can include logo placements on team jerseys, mentions in social media posts, and branding in live streams and tournament broadcasts.

For example, a team sponsored by a hardware manufacturer might use and promote their products during competitions. In return, the sponsor gets visibility every time the team competes or engages with their fan base. This mutually beneficial relationship helps teams cover expenses like player salaries, travel, and training facilities, while sponsors gain access to a dedicated and engaged audience.

The Role of Advertising

Advertising in eSports goes beyond traditional sponsorships. The digital nature of eSports offers unique advertising opportunities that are not possible in conventional sports. Live streaming platforms like Twitch and YouTube Gaming have become prime real estate for advertisers looking to reach eSports audiences.

These platforms offer various advertising formats, including pre-roll ads (videos that play before a stream starts), mid-roll ads (videos that play during breaks in a stream), and banner ads displayed on the stream page. Streamers themselves can also engage in direct advertising by promoting products during their broadcasts, often through sponsored segments or product placements.

The interactivity of live streaming allows for more engaging advertising experiences. Viewers can click on ads to get more information or make purchases, making the advertising experience more seamless and effective.

T1's Valorant Team Wearing Branded Jerseys Sponsored by Major Companies. Source: bleedingcool.com

The Impact of Sponsorship and Advertising on eSports Growth

The influx of sponsorship and advertising money has been a game-changer for eSports. It has allowed for larger prize pools, more professional team infrastructures, and the ability to host high-quality events that rival traditional sports in production value. This financial support has also enabled players to pursue gaming as a full-time career, leading to higher levels of competition and more engaging content for fans.

One of the most significant impacts has been the professionalization of the industry. With stable financial backing, teams can invest in training facilities, coaching staff, and player development. This has raised the overall skill level within eSports and helped attract more viewers, further fueling the growth cycle.

Moreover, the visibility brought by major brands entering the space has helped eSports gain mainstream recognition. Large-scale sponsorship deals with companies like Intel, Coca-Cola, and Mercedes-Benz have legitimized eSports in the eyes of the broader public and opened the door for even more investment.

Challenges and Future Trends

While sponsorship and advertising have driven much of the growth in eSports, the industry still faces challenges. One significant issue is the volatility of sponsorship deals. Brands may enter and exit the space quickly, leading to financial instability for teams and players. Additionally, as the industry grows, there is increasing competition for sponsorship dollars, making it harder for smaller teams to secure deals.

Looking ahead, the future of sponsorship and advertising in eSports appears promising. As the audience continues to grow and diversify, more brands are likely to invest in the space. Innovations in technology, such as augmented reality (AR) and virtual reality (VR), may also open new avenues for immersive advertising experiences.

Furthermore, as eSports becomes more integrated with traditional sports, we may see crossover sponsorship deals that leverage the strengths of both industries. The potential for growth in eSports sponsorship and advertising is vast, and it will be exciting to see how the landscape evolves in the coming years.

Sponsorship and advertising have been crucial in transforming eSports into the global phenomenon it is today. These financial pillars have enabled the professionalization of teams, the enhancement of viewer experiences, and the overall growth of the industry. As eSports continues to expand, the role of sponsorship and advertising will undoubtedly remain central to its success.

Monetizing Content

Monetizing content in the eSports industry has become a cornerstone of financial success for both individual creators and organizations. The ability to generate revenue from various forms of content has opened up numerous opportunities, allowing eSports to thrive beyond just competitive play.

Streaming Platforms

One of the most effective ways to monetize content is through streaming platforms like Twitch and YouTube. These platforms allow players and content creators to broadcast their gameplay to a global audience. Viewers can watch live streams or on-demand videos, engaging with the content in real-time through comments and live chats.

Revenue from streaming comes from several sources. Advertisements play before or during streams, providing a steady income. Subscriptions are another significant revenue stream. Fans can subscribe to their favorite channels for a monthly fee, often receiving perks like exclusive content or ad-free viewing. Additionally, viewers can donate money directly to streamers during live broadcasts, often accompanied by a personalized message or shout-out.

Sponsorships and Partnerships

Sponsorships and partnerships are critical in content monetization. Brands recognize the influence of popular streamers and content creators, and they are willing to pay for exposure to their audiences. These deals can range from sponsored segments and product placements to long-term partnerships.

For instance, a gaming hardware company might sponsor a streamer by providing them with the latest equipment, which the streamer then uses and promotes during their broadcasts. These sponsorships not only provide financial support but also add credibility and professional polish to the content.

Advertisements

Advertisements are a straightforward way to monetize content. On platforms like YouTube, ads are placed before, during, or after videos. Creators earn a share of the ad revenue based on the number of views and clicks. The more popular the content, the higher the ad revenue.

In addition to traditional ads, content creators can integrate sponsored messages or product placements within their videos. This method often feels more organic and can be more engaging for the audience. Creators who successfully blend advertising with their content can create a seamless experience that benefits both the advertiser and the viewer.

Affiliate Marketing

Affiliate marketing is another effective strategy. Content creators can promote products or services through unique affiliate links. When viewers click these links and make purchases, the creator earns a commission. This model works well for gaming peripherals, software, and other related products.

For example, a streamer might provide a link to the gaming mouse they use, encouraging viewers to purchase it through their affiliate link. This approach not only generates income but also provides value to the audience by recommending quality products.

Merchandise

Selling merchandise is a popular way to monetize content. Streamers and content creators often design and sell branded merchandise such as T-shirts, hoodies, mugs, and other accessories. These items allow fans to show their support and feel more connected to their favorite creators.

Merchandise sales can be managed through online stores, often integrated with the creator's channel or website. Special limited-edition items or collaborations with popular brands can drive higher sales and create additional buzz.

Premium Content

Offering premium content is another lucrative model. Content creators can provide exclusive videos, early access to new content, or behind-the-scenes footage to fans who pay a subscription fee. Platforms like Patreon facilitate this by allowing creators to set up membership tiers with different levels of access and perks.

Premium content not only generates additional revenue but also fosters a closer relationship with dedicated fans. Those who are willing to pay for exclusive content are often the most engaged and supportive members of the audience.

Crowdfunding

Crowdfunding platforms like Kickstarter or GoFundMe provide another avenue for monetizing content. Content creators can launch campaigns to fund specific projects, such as new video series, equipment upgrades, or event coverage. Fans contribute financially to support these initiatives, often receiving rewards or recognition in return.

Crowdfunding allows creators to undertake more ambitious projects without the immediate financial pressure, while also engaging their community in the process.

Events and Live Appearances

Beyond digital content, live events and appearances can be monetized effectively. Streamers and content creators often participate in gaming conventions, eSports tournaments, and fan meet-and-greets. These events can include ticket sales, exclusive merchandise, and sponsored segments, all contributing to overall revenue.

Live appearances provide a unique opportunity for creators to interact with their audience in person, strengthening the community and expanding their reach.

Monetizing content in eSports involves a multifaceted approach, leveraging various revenue streams to create a sustainable and profitable career. Streaming platforms, sponsorships, advertisements, affiliate marketing, merchandise, premium content, crowdfunding, and live events all play a part in this ecosystem. Each method offers unique opportunities and challenges, and successful content creators often blend several strategies to maximize their earnings and maintain a strong connection with their audience.

Chapter 3: Technology and Innovation

The Evolution of Gaming Hardware

The evolution of gaming hardware has been a critical factor in the rise of eSports. From the earliest arcade machines to the high-performance gaming rigs of today, advancements in technology have continually pushed the boundaries of what is possible in competitive gaming. This section explores the key developments in gaming hardware and how they have shaped the eSports landscape.

The Early Days: Arcade Machines and Consoles

The journey of gaming hardware began with arcade machines in the late 1970s and early 1980s. Games like "Space Invaders," "Pac-Man," and "Donkey Kong" captured the public's imagination, with their coin-operated cabinets becoming a staple in arcades worldwide. These machines were marvels of engineering for their time, featuring custom-built hardware designed to run specific games efficiently.

Home consoles soon followed, bringing the gaming experience into living rooms. The release of the Atari 2600 in 1977 marked the beginning of console gaming. It was succeeded by other iconic systems like the Nintendo Entertainment System (NES) in 1983 and the Sega Genesis in 1988. These consoles made gaming more accessible and fostered the development of competitive play among friends and family.

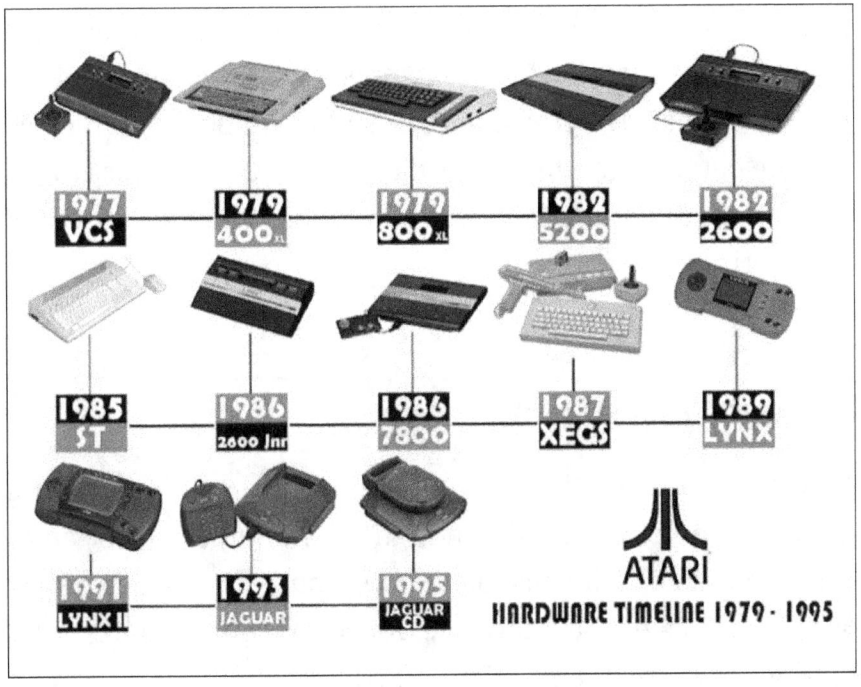

The ATARI Consoles Timeline. Source: sify.com

The Rise of Personal Computers

As personal computers (PCs) became more affordable and powerful, they started to play a significant role in gaming. The 1990s saw the rise of PC gaming, with titles like "Doom," "Quake," and "StarCraft" paving the way for eSports. PCs offered greater flexibility and performance compared to consoles, allowing for more complex and graphically intensive games.

One of the major advancements during this period was the introduction of dedicated graphics cards. Companies like NVIDIA and ATI (now AMD) developed GPUs that significantly improved rendering performance, enabling smoother gameplay and more detailed graphics. This hardware evolution was crucial for games that required fast, precise actions, which are essential in competitive gaming.

The Impact of the Internet

The widespread adoption of the internet in the late 1990s and early 2000s revolutionized gaming. Online multiplayer games became possible, allowing players to compete against others worldwide. This era saw the emergence of iconic eSports titles like "Counter-Strike" and "Warcraft III."

To support online gaming, PCs needed robust networking capabilities and sufficient processing power to handle real-time data. Broadband internet connections and improved networking hardware made it feasible for players to participate in online tournaments, setting the stage for the modern eSports ecosystem.

The Modern Era: High-Performance Gaming

Today's gaming hardware is a far cry from the early days of arcade machines and 8-bit consoles. Modern gaming PCs are equipped with multi-core processors, high-speed RAM, and powerful GPUs capable of rendering ultra-high-definition graphics. This hardware provides the performance needed for modern eSports titles like "Fortnite," "League of Legends," and "Dota 2."

Peripheral devices have also seen significant advancements. Mechanical keyboards, high-DPI mice, and low-latency monitors give players the precision and responsiveness required for competitive play. Additionally, innovations like VR headsets and haptic feedback devices are beginning to offer more immersive gaming experiences.

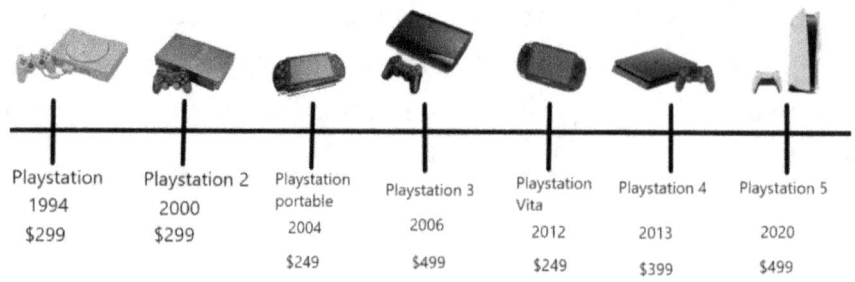

Playstation	Playstation 2	Playstation portable	Playstation 3	Playstation Vita	Playstation 4	Playstation 5
1994	2000	2004	2006	2012	2013	2020
$299	$299	$249	$499	$249	$399	$499

The PlayStation Consoles Timeline. Source: reddit.com

The Role of Gaming Laptops

While desktop PCs dominate the eSports scene, gaming laptops have become increasingly popular. Modern gaming laptops feature high-end components in portable form factors, allowing players to compete from anywhere. Advances in cooling technology and power management have made it possible to pack desktop-level performance into these devices.

Customization and Optimization

One of the hallmarks of modern gaming hardware is the ability to customize and optimize. Enthusiasts can build custom PCs tailored to their specific needs, selecting components that offer the best performance for their preferred games. Overclocking, a practice where users increase the clock rate of their components, allows for even greater performance gains.

Software optimization is also crucial. Game developers work closely with hardware manufacturers to ensure their games run smoothly on a wide range of systems. Tools like NVIDIA's GeForce Experience and AMD's Radeon Software provide drivers and settings optimizations to enhance performance.

The Future of Gaming Hardware

The evolution of gaming hardware shows no signs of slowing down. Emerging technologies like ray tracing, which simulates realistic lighting effects, are pushing graphical fidelity to new heights. The development of quantum computing and AI-driven gaming engines holds the promise of even more revolutionary changes.

Cloud gaming services like Google Stadia and NVIDIA GeForce Now are also on the rise. These platforms allow players to stream games from powerful remote servers, reducing the need for high-end local hardware. This technology could make competitive gaming more accessible by lowering the entry barrier for high-performance gaming.

The journey from simple arcade machines to today's cutting-edge gaming PCs has been remarkable. Each advancement in hardware has opened new possibilities for games and has been instrumental in the growth of eSports. As technology continues to evolve, it will be exciting to see how the next generation of hardware will shape the future of competitive gaming.

Streaming Platforms and Their Impact

Streaming platforms have revolutionized the way we consume and engage with eSports content. Platforms like Twitch, YouTube Gaming, and Facebook Gaming have not only provided a stage for gamers to showcase their skills but have also created vibrant communities around eSports. The impact of these platforms on the industry is profound and multifaceted.

The Rise of Twitch

Twitch, launched in 2011, quickly became the leading platform for live streaming video games. Its user-friendly interface and interactive features made it a favorite among gamers and viewers alike. Twitch offered a new way for players to broadcast their gameplay in real-time, allowing fans to watch, chat, and interact with streamers.

The platform's success can be attributed to its focus on community engagement. Twitch's chat feature allows viewers to communicate directly with streamers and other fans, creating a sense of community and immediacy. This interaction fosters loyalty and keeps viewers coming back for more.

Twitch's impact on eSports has been significant. Major tournaments and events are streamed live, attracting millions of viewers worldwide. This visibility has helped elevate eSports to a mainstream audience, bringing in sponsors and advertisers eager to reach this engaged demographic.

Twitch Streaming Setup. Source: obsbot.com

YouTube Gaming and the Power of Video Content

YouTube, already a giant in online video content, launched YouTube Gaming in 2015 to capitalize on the growing popularity of game streaming. While it didn't overtake Twitch, YouTube Gaming has carved out its niche by leveraging YouTube's massive user base and robust video platform.

The strength of YouTube Gaming lies in its versatility. Streamers can live broadcast their games and upload pre-recorded content, highlights, tutorials, and more. This combination of live and on-demand content has broadened the reach of eSports, making it accessible to a wider audience.

YouTube's sophisticated recommendation algorithms also help in discovering new content, driving traffic to lesser-known streamers and expanding their audiences. This has democratized content creation, allowing more players to find their place in the eSports ecosystem.

Facebook Gaming: Social Integration

Facebook Gaming entered the scene with a unique advantage: integration with the world's largest social media network. Launched in 2018, Facebook Gaming aims to make game streaming more social by leveraging Facebook's extensive user base and social features.

The platform allows users to easily share streams with their friends and join gaming communities. This social integration helps in building a more connected and engaged audience. Facebook Gaming also benefits from the platform's robust ad network, providing additional revenue opportunities for streamers through in-stream ads and fan support.

Facebook's push into eSports has brought new viewers into the fold, particularly those who might not be traditional gaming enthusiasts. This broadens the demographic reach of eSports, helping it to grow beyond its core audience.

Creating Opportunities for Gamers

Streaming platforms have created unprecedented opportunities for gamers. Talented players no longer need to rely solely on professional teams or tournament winnings to make a living. They can build their own brands and monetize their content through donations, subscriptions, and sponsorships.

This shift has led to the rise of the "streamer" as a profession. Streamers like Ninja, Shroud, and Pokimane have become household names, earning substantial incomes from their online presence. Their success stories inspire others to pursue careers in gaming and content creation.

Moreover, streaming platforms have democratized the eSports landscape. Players from all over the world, regardless of their background or location, can broadcast their gameplay and reach a global audience. This inclusivity has enriched the eSports community, bringing in diverse voices and talents.

Impact on eSports Viewership

The advent of streaming platforms has dramatically increased eSports viewership. Major events that were once confined to physical venues can now be watched by millions of fans around the world. This accessibility has propelled eSports into the mainstream, attracting viewers who might not have attended live events.

Live streaming also adds an element of excitement and immediacy to eSports. Fans can watch matches as they happen, participate in live chats, and even influence the content through donations and interactions. This level of engagement is unique to the digital space and enhances the overall viewing experience.

Fostering Community and Engagement

Streaming platforms excel at fostering community and engagement. Features like live chat, subscriber-only content, and community events help build strong connections between streamers and their audiences. Viewers feel like they are part of a community, sharing their passion for gaming with like-minded individuals.

These communities often extend beyond the streams themselves. Fans join Discord servers, social media groups, and online forums to discuss their favorite games and streamers. This sense of belonging is a powerful driver of loyalty and engagement.

Driving Innovation and Content Diversity

The competitive nature of streaming platforms has driven innovation in content creation. Streamers are constantly experimenting with new formats, from interactive streams and game reviews to collaborative events and charity fundraisers. This creativity keeps the content fresh and exciting, attracting new viewers and retaining existing ones.

The diversity of content on streaming platforms also contributes to their appeal. Viewers can find streams for virtually any game or genre, catering to a wide range of interests. This variety ensures that there is something for everyone, further expanding the audience for eSports.

Streaming platforms have fundamentally transformed the eSports landscape. They have provided a stage for gamers to showcase their skills, created new revenue streams, and built vibrant communities around gaming. As these platforms continue to evolve, their impact on eSports will only grow, further solidifying gaming's place in the world of entertainment.

Emerging Technologies

The eSports industry is constantly evolving, driven by rapid advancements in technology. Emerging technologies are not only enhancing the gaming experience but also transforming the way games are played, watched, and monetized. This section explores some of the most promising emerging technologies that are set to shape the future of eSports.

Virtual Reality

Virtual Reality (VR) is one of the most exciting developments in gaming technology. VR creates immersive environments that allow players to experience games in a completely new way.

Instead of viewing the game on a screen, players are transported into a three-dimensional world where they can interact with their surroundings.

In eSports, VR has the potential to revolutionize both player experience and spectator engagement. Games like "Beat Saber" and "Echo Arena" are early examples of competitive VR games that offer a glimpse into the future. VR tournaments could become a staple in eSports, providing audiences with unique, immersive viewing experiences.

VR City. Source: vrcity.ch

Augmented Reality

While VR immerses players in a completely virtual world, Augmented Reality (AR) overlays digital information onto the real world. This technology can enhance gaming by blending virtual elements with the physical environment.

In eSports, AR can be used to enhance live events. Imagine attending a tournament where you can see real-time stats and player information projected onto the arena. AR can also be used in training, allowing players to visualize strategies and practice in a more interactive way.

5G Technology

The rollout of 5G technology promises to bring significant improvements to online gaming. With faster speeds, lower latency, and more reliable connections, 5G will enable smoother and more responsive gameplay. This is particularly important for eSports, where split-second decisions can determine the outcome of a match.

5G can also enhance mobile gaming, making high-quality competitive gaming accessible on smartphones and tablets. This could lead to the rise of mobile eSports, expanding the audience and player base even further.

Artificial Intelligence

Artificial Intelligence (AI) is already making an impact in game development and player training. AI can be used to create more intelligent and challenging non-player characters (NPCs), providing better practice environments for players. AI-driven analytics can also help players improve their performance by analyzing gameplay and offering personalized recommendations.

In addition, AI can enhance the spectator experience. Machine learning algorithms can predict match outcomes, highlight key moments, and provide insightful commentary, making the viewing experience more engaging and informative.

Blockchain and NFTs

Blockchain technology and Non-Fungible Tokens (NFTs) are emerging as innovative solutions for in-game economies and digital asset ownership. Blockchain can ensure the security and transparency of transactions, making in-game purchases and trades more reliable.

NFTs allow players to own unique digital items, such as skins, weapons, or even characters, that can be bought, sold, or traded.

This opens up new possibilities for monetization in eSports, where players and fans can invest in and collect valuable digital assets.

Cloud Gaming

Cloud gaming services like Google Stadia, NVIDIA GeForce Now, and Microsoft's Xbox Cloud Gaming are changing the way games are accessed and played. Instead of requiring powerful local hardware, cloud gaming allows players to stream games from remote servers. This makes high-quality gaming more accessible and affordable.

For eSports, cloud gaming can democratize participation by lowering the barrier to entry. Players with less powerful hardware can still compete at a high level, broadening the competitive landscape and attracting new talent.

Advanced Streaming Technologies

The way eSports are broadcasted is also evolving with emerging streaming technologies. Low-latency streaming, 4K resolution, and interactive features are enhancing the viewer experience. Platforms like Twitch and YouTube Gaming are constantly innovating to provide better quality streams and more engaging content.

Interactive features, such as real-time polls, chat integrations, and viewer-controlled camera angles, make watching eSports more interactive and personalized. These advancements are helping to grow the audience and increase viewer engagement.

Wearable Technology

Wearable technology, such as smartwatches and fitness trackers, is becoming more integrated into the gaming world. These devices can monitor a player's physical condition, providing real-time data on heart rate, stress levels, and other vital signs. This information can be used to optimize performance and manage stress during competitions.

In professional eSports, wearables can also help coaches and analysts develop better training regimens and strategies tailored to individual players' needs.

The rapid pace of technological innovation is continually reshaping the eSports landscape. Virtual Reality, Augmented Reality, 5G, AI, blockchain, cloud gaming, advanced streaming technologies, and wearable technology are just a few of the emerging trends that hold the potential to revolutionize the industry. As these technologies develop and become more integrated into the world of eSports, they will open up new possibilities for players, teams, and audiences alike. The future of eSports looks brighter than ever, with technology driving the next wave of growth and innovation.

Chapter 4: The Economics of eSports

Market Size and Growth Trends

The eSports industry has seen explosive growth over the past decade, evolving from a niche market into a significant player in the global entertainment landscape. Understanding the market size and growth trends helps illustrate the rapid expansion and the potential future trajectory of this dynamic sector.

Rapid Market Expansion

The global eSports market has experienced a remarkable surge in value. In 2019, the market was valued at approximately $1.1 billion. By 2022, it surpassed $1.7 billion, with projections suggesting it could reach 11.94 billion by 2030. This growth is driven by increasing viewership, rising investments, and expanding revenue streams.

The number of eSports enthusiasts worldwide has also grown significantly. In 2020, the global audience for eSports was around 495 million. This number is grown to 646 million by

2023. The increasing accessibility of online platforms and the proliferation of mobile gaming have played crucial roles in broadening the audience base.

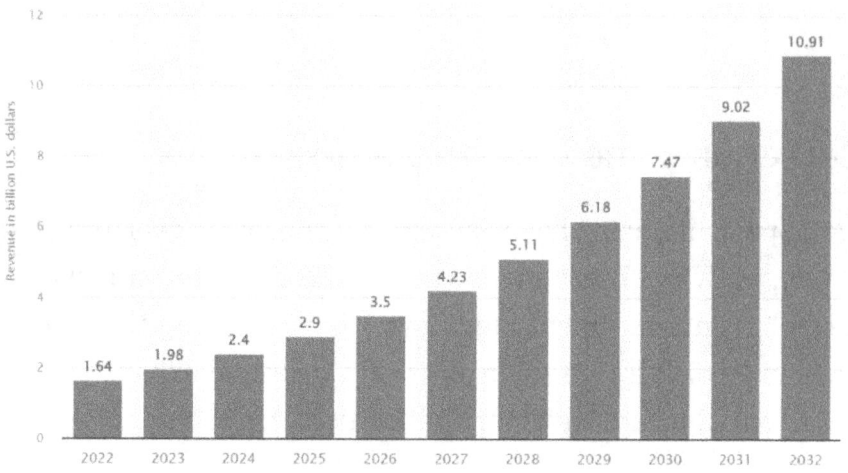

Size of Global eSports Market 2022-2032 (revenue in billion U.S. dollars). Source: statista.com

Key Revenue Streams

Several revenue streams contribute to the financial health of the eSports industry. Sponsorship remains the largest source of income, accounting for approximately 40% of total revenue. Brands are keen to tap into the young, engaged audience that eSports commands, leading to lucrative sponsorship deals and partnerships.

Media rights represent another significant revenue stream. Broadcasting deals with platforms like Twitch, YouTube, and traditional TV networks have brought substantial income to the industry. As viewership numbers climb, the value of these media rights continues to increase.

Merchandise and ticket sales, although impacted by the COVID-19 pandemic, are rebounding as live events return. Fans are eager to attend tournaments and purchase branded merchandise, contributing to the overall revenue.

Geographical Growth

The growth of eSports is a global phenomenon, with significant regional variations. Asia, particularly China and South Korea, remains the largest market, driven by a deep-rooted gaming culture and strong infrastructure for competitive gaming. China's eSports market alone is surpass $400 million by 2023.

North America and Europe also represent substantial markets, with growing investments and increasing audience numbers. The North American market is reach $300 million by 2023, while Europe is hit $200 million. Both regions benefit from strong media partnerships and a robust infrastructure for hosting major events.

Emerging markets like Latin America and Southeast Asia are also experiencing rapid growth. These regions are seeing increased investments and a rising number of local tournaments and leagues, indicating their potential as future powerhouses in the eSports industry.

Investment and Mergers

The eSports industry has attracted significant investment from venture capitalists, traditional sports teams, and entertainment companies. These investments are fueling the development of new teams, leagues, and infrastructure. Major corporations like Comcast, Disney, and Tencent have made substantial investments, recognizing the potential of eSports to generate long-term returns.

Mergers and acquisitions are becoming more common as well. Established eSports organizations are acquiring smaller teams and content creators to expand their reach and diversify their revenue streams. This consolidation is helping to professionalize the industry and attract further investment.

Technological Advancements

Technological advancements are playing a critical role in the growth of eSports. High-speed internet, advanced gaming hardware, and streaming platforms have made it easier for fans to watch and participate in eSports. Virtual reality and augmented reality technologies are also beginning to make their mark, offering new ways to experience gaming.

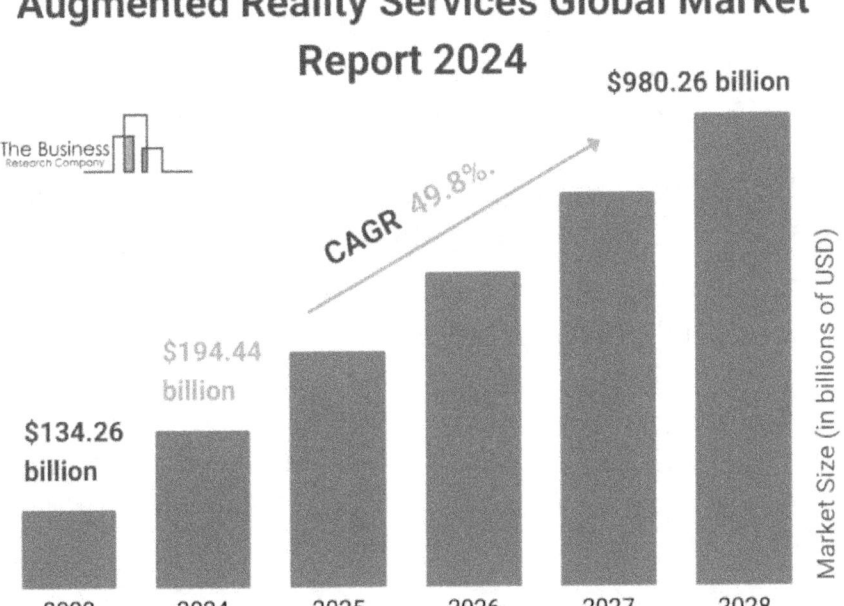

Augmented Reality ServicesMarket Size 2024 And Growth Rate.
Source: thebusinessresearchcompany.com

Blockchain technology and cryptocurrencies are emerging trends within the eSports industry. These technologies are being used to enhance security, facilitate microtransactions, and create new opportunities for fan engagement through digital collectibles and tokens.

Mobile Gaming

The rise of mobile gaming is a significant trend driving the growth of eSports. Mobile games like "Honor of Kings," "PUBG Mobile," and "Free Fire" have massive player bases and viewership numbers. The accessibility of mobile gaming has opened up eSports to a broader audience, particularly in regions with less access to high-end gaming PCs or consoles.

Mobile eSports tournaments are becoming more frequent and prestigious, with substantial prize pools and international participation. This trend is expected to continue, further fueling the growth of the eSports market.

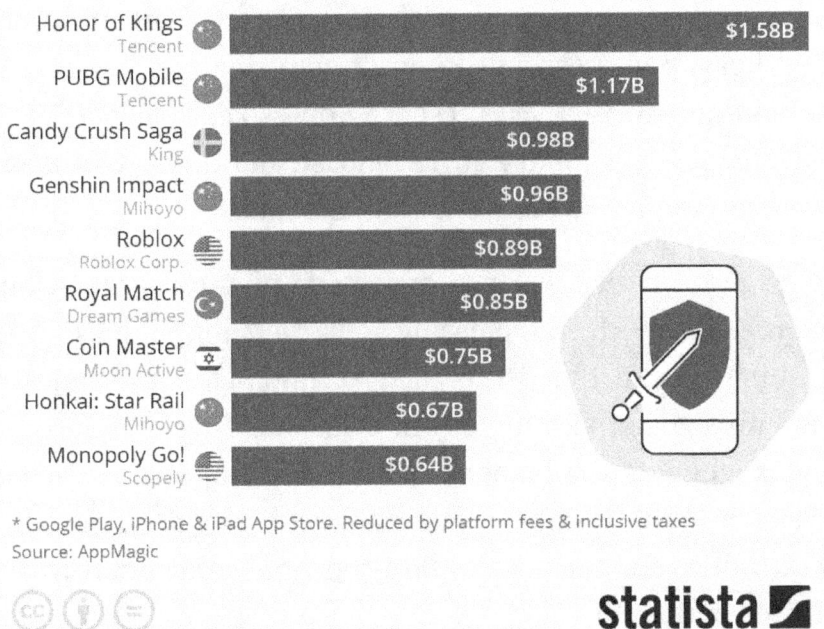

How Lucrative Is Gaming on the Go?

Mobile games with the highest estimated revenue in 2023*

Honor of Kings (Tencent)		$1.58B
PUBG Mobile (Tencent)		$1.17B
Candy Crush Saga (King)		$0.98B
Genshin Impact (Mihoyo)		$0.96B
Roblox (Roblox Corp.)		$0.89B
Royal Match (Dream Games)		$0.85B
Coin Master (Moon Active)		$0.75B
Honkai: Star Rail (Mihoyo)		$0.67B
Monopoly Go! (Scopely)		$0.64B

* Google Play, iPhone & iPad App Store. Reduced by platform fees & inclusive taxes
Source: AppMagic

statista

The Most Successful Mobile Games of 2023. Source: statista.com

Social Media and Community Engagement

Social media platforms have become essential tools for eSports organizations to engage with their audience. Platforms like X,

Instagram, and TikTok provide real-time interaction and content sharing, enhancing fan engagement and loyalty. These platforms also offer additional revenue opportunities through sponsored content and advertisements.

Community engagement is critical in eSports. Organizations invest heavily in creating content, organizing fan events, and maintaining an active presence on social media. This engagement helps build a loyal fanbase and drives consistent viewership for live streams and tournaments.

The eSports market is on a trajectory of rapid growth and expansion. With increasing viewership, substantial investments, and the rise of new technologies, the industry shows no signs of slowing down. Understanding these growth trends highlights the immense potential of eSports as a major player in the global entertainment landscape, with opportunities for further development and innovation in the years to come.

Investment in eSports

The eSports industry has witnessed a surge in investment over the past decade, transforming it from a niche hobby into a mainstream phenomenon. This influx of capital has been crucial in professionalizing the sector, driving innovation, and expanding its reach globally. In this section, we explore the various facets of investment in eSports, including venture capital, corporate sponsorships, and the impact of these investments on the industry's growth.

The Rise of Venture Capital

Venture capital has played a significant role in the growth of eSports. Investors have recognized the potential of this burgeoning industry, leading to substantial funding for teams, tournament organizers, and related businesses. Early investments were often driven by a belief in the future of digital entertainment and the growing popularity of competitive gaming.

One notable example is the investment in professional eSports organizations such as Cloud9 and Team Liquid. These organizations have received millions of dollars in funding to support their operations, including player salaries, training facilities, and marketing efforts. Such investments have enabled these teams to compete at the highest levels and attract global audiences.

Venture capital has also flowed into startups developing eSports infrastructure, such as streaming platforms, analytics tools, and gaming peripherals. Companies like Twitch, which Amazon acquired for nearly $1 billion in 2014, exemplify the lucrative potential of investments in eSports-related technology.

Corporate Sponsorships and Partnerships

Corporate sponsorships are another major source of investment in eSports. Brands across various industries have recognized the value of associating with eSports to reach a young, engaged audience. Sponsorship deals provide essential funding for teams and events, while brands benefit from increased visibility and consumer engagement.

Tech companies, beverage brands, and automotive manufacturers are among the most active sponsors in eSports. For instance, Intel's partnership with ESL (Electronic Sports League) has been pivotal in hosting and promoting major tournaments like the Intel Extreme Masters. Similarly, Red Bull sponsors several eSports athletes and events, enhancing its brand presence in the gaming community.

These partnerships often extend beyond financial support. Sponsors may provide products, promotional activities, and expertise to enhance the eSports experience. This symbiotic relationship helps elevate the quality of competitions and brings additional value to both parties.

The Impact of Franchise Models

The introduction of franchise models in leagues such as the Overwatch League (OWL) and the League of Legends Championship Series (LCS) has attracted significant investment from traditional sports team owners and media companies. These franchise systems offer a more stable and scalable structure for the industry, similar to traditional sports leagues.

Investors purchase franchise slots for substantial sums, securing their place in the league and gaining access to revenue sharing, media rights, and merchandising opportunities. This model provides financial stability for teams and encourages long-term investment in the growth of the league.

For example, the OWL's franchise slots sold for $20 million to $60 million each, drawing investment from NBA, NFL, and MLB team owners. This influx of capital has been used to develop local fan bases, improve production quality, and enhance player welfare, contributing to the overall growth and sustainability of the league.

Media Rights and Broadcasting Deals

Media rights and broadcasting deals have emerged as significant revenue streams in eSports, attracting investment from major media companies. These deals involve the exclusive rights to stream and broadcast eSports events, providing a steady income for organizers and increasing the visibility of eSports.

Platforms like Twitch, YouTube Gaming, and Facebook Gaming have secured exclusive broadcasting rights for various tournaments, while traditional sports networks such as ESPN and TBS have also entered the fray. These deals are often lucrative, reflecting the growing audience and commercial potential of eSports.

In 2020, Riot Games secured a multi-year deal with Chinese streaming platform Bilibili for exclusive broadcasting rights to the League of Legends World Championship in China, reportedly worth $113 million. Such deals highlight the increasing value of eSports content and the willingness of media companies to invest heavily in the sector.

The Role of Crowdfunding

Crowdfunding has also become a popular method of raising funds in the eSports industry. Platforms like Kickstarter and Patreon allow fans to directly support their favorite teams, players, and projects. This grassroots funding approach can be particularly effective for smaller teams and content creators seeking to build a loyal following.

Crowdfunding not only provides financial support but also fosters a sense of community and engagement among fans. Successful campaigns often offer exclusive rewards and experiences, creating a deeper connection between supporters and the eSports entities they back.

Challenges and Considerations

While investment in eSports has been largely positive, it comes with its challenges. The industry is still relatively young and rapidly evolving, which can lead to volatility and uncertainty. Investors must navigate issues such as fluctuating viewership, regulatory changes, and the need for sustainable business models.

Moreover, the intense competition for sponsorship dollars and media rights means that not all investments will yield high returns. Due diligence and a thorough understanding of the eSports ecosystem are crucial for making informed investment decisions.

Investment in eSports has been a driving force behind the industry's rapid growth and professionalization. From venture capital and corporate sponsorships to franchise models and media rights deals, various forms of investment have helped shape the modern eSports landscape. As the industry continues to expand, these investments will play a vital role in its ongoing development and success.

Economic Challenges and Opportunities

The eSports industry, while experiencing rapid growth and popularity, faces a number of economic challenges. However, these challenges are accompanied by significant opportunities that can drive further expansion and innovation in the sector. Understanding these dynamics is essential for stakeholders looking to navigate the complexities of the eSports economy.

Revenue Diversification

One of the primary challenges in eSports is the reliance on a limited number of revenue streams, such as sponsorships, advertising, and media rights. While these streams are lucrative, the industry needs to diversify its income sources to ensure long-term sustainability. The potential for growth in areas like merchandise sales, ticketing for live events, and direct-to-consumer content is immense. Organizations that successfully tap into these additional revenue streams can create more robust financial models and reduce dependency on any single source of income.

Sponsorship Saturation

Sponsorships are a significant revenue driver for eSports, but there is a risk of market saturation. As more brands enter the space, the competition for sponsorship deals intensifies, potentially driving down the value of individual agreements. This saturation can also lead to over-commercialization, which might alienate core audiences. To mitigate this, eSports organizations need to innovate in their sponsorship approaches, offering unique and tailored packages that deliver tangible value to sponsors while maintaining authenticity with their audience.

Player Salaries and Team Expenses

The increasing popularity of eSports has led to rising player salaries and team operational costs. While high salaries attract top talent, they also put financial pressure on organizations, particularly those without substantial backing or diverse revenue streams. Managing these costs requires careful financial planning and strategic investment. Opportunities lie in creating sustainable business models that balance player compensation with organizational growth, possibly through revenue-sharing arrangements and performance-based incentives.

Infrastructure and Logistics

Hosting live eSports events involves significant logistical challenges, including venue selection, technological infrastructure, and audience management. These events can be expensive to organize and require substantial upfront investment. However, the opportunity to create memorable, large-scale events that attract global audiences and media attention is immense. Leveraging partnerships with established event organizers and investing in state-of-the-art infrastructure can help overcome these challenges and enhance the fan experience.

Regulatory and Legal Issues

The eSports industry faces a complex regulatory landscape, with varying laws and regulations across different regions. Issues such as gambling laws, player contracts, and intellectual property rights can create legal hurdles. Staying compliant with these regulations is essential, but it also presents an opportunity for standardization and professionalization within the industry. Establishing clear guidelines and working with regulatory bodies can help create a more stable and predictable environment for all stakeholders.

Market Penetration and Global Expansion

While eSports has a strong presence in regions like North America, Europe, and Asia, there are still untapped markets with significant potential. Expanding into these regions involves understanding local cultures, preferences, and regulatory environments. The opportunity to grow the global eSports audience is vast, and organizations that successfully penetrate new markets can capitalize on fresh streams of revenue and fan engagement. Developing localized content, partnering with regional influencers, and investing in grassroots initiatives can drive this expansion.

Technology and Innovation

Rapid technological advancements present both challenges and opportunities for the eSports industry. Staying at the forefront of technology requires continuous investment in the latest gaming hardware, software, and broadcasting tools. However, embracing new technologies such as virtual reality, augmented reality, and blockchain can create innovative experiences for fans and new revenue opportunities. Organizations that invest in technology and innovation can differentiate themselves and offer unique value propositions to their audiences.

Audience Engagement and Retention

Maintaining and growing an engaged audience is crucial for the long-term success of eSports. The industry must continually find ways to captivate viewers and keep them returning. This challenge is met with opportunities in content creation, interactive experiences, and personalized fan engagement. Leveraging data analytics to understand viewer preferences and behaviors can help tailor content and marketing strategies. Additionally, fostering strong community ties through social media, live events, and exclusive content can enhance audience loyalty.

Economic Sustainability

Ensuring economic sustainability in eSports involves creating business models that can withstand market fluctuations and economic downturns. Diversifying income sources, investing in talent development, and building strong brand identities are key strategies. The opportunity lies in adopting a holistic approach to business development, focusing on long-term growth rather than short-term gains. By doing so, organizations can build resilient operations capable of thriving in a dynamic and competitive landscape.

The eSports industry is at a pivotal point, balancing significant economic challenges with tremendous opportunities for growth and innovation. By addressing these challenges strategically, stakeholders can harness the full potential of eSports, driving the industry forward into a new era of success and sustainability.

Chapter 5: The Cultural Phenomenon

The Rise of eSports Fandom

The explosion of eSports fandom is one of the most remarkable phenomena in modern entertainment. What began as small groups of enthusiasts gathering in arcades and online forums has evolved into a global community of millions, passionately following their favorite games, teams, and players. This section explores the factors that have fueled the rise of eSports fandom, the characteristics of this diverse fan base, and the impact it has had on the industry.

The Early Days of eSports Fandom

In the early days, eSports fandom was a niche culture. Enthusiasts would gather in person at local arcades or internet cafes to compete and watch others play. Online forums and message boards became the first virtual meeting places for fans, where they could discuss strategies, share tips, and celebrate their favorite games.

These early communities were tightly knit and driven by a shared passion for gaming. Events like the QuakeCon and the Evolution Championship Series (EVO) began to draw attention, creating a sense of legitimacy and excitement around competitive gaming. As broadband internet became more accessible, the ability to watch live streams of gameplay over the internet helped eSports reach a broader audience.

The Impact of Live Streaming

The advent of live streaming platforms like Twitch and YouTube Gaming revolutionized eSports fandom. These platforms allowed fans to watch live broadcasts of games and tournaments from anywhere in the world, breaking down geographical barriers and creating a truly global fan base.

Live streaming also provided a way for fans to interact with their favorite players and content creators in real-time. Chat features enabled viewers to engage with each other and the streamer, fostering a sense of community and connection. This direct interaction has been pivotal in building loyal fan bases and creating personal connections between players and their audiences.

Moreover, the accessibility of live streaming has democratized content creation. Aspiring gamers can broadcast their gameplay and build their own followings, contributing to the growth of eSports culture. This has led to a diverse array of content, from high-level competitive play to casual gaming and educational streams.

The Role of Social Media

Social media has played an instrumental role in the rise of eSports fandom. Platforms like X, Facebook, Instagram, and Reddit allow fans to stay up-to-date with the latest news, interact with their favorite teams and players, and participate in discussions about their favorite games.

Teams and players use social media to share behind-the-scenes content, announce events, and engage with their supporters. This constant stream of content keeps fans engaged and invested in the eSports ecosystem. Hashtags, fan pages, and community groups have also helped organize and amplify the voices of eSports fans, making it easier to rally support and build excitement around events.

Major Tournaments and Live Events

Major eSports tournaments and live events have been crucial in solidifying eSports fandom. Events like The International, the League of Legends World Championship, and the Overwatch League Grand Finals attract millions of viewers and thousands of live attendees. These events are not just competitions; they are spectacles with high production values, celebrity appearances, and fan activities.

The atmosphere at live events is electric, with fans donning team jerseys, waving banners, and chanting for their favorite players. These gatherings create a sense of camaraderie and shared experience, much like traditional sports events. The excitement and energy of these events have helped convert casual viewers into dedicated fans.

The Diversity of eSports Fans

One of the most striking aspects of eSports fandom is its diversity. eSports fans come from all walks of life, spanning different ages, genders, and cultural backgrounds. This diversity is reflected in the wide range of games that cater to various interests, from strategy games like "StarCraft" to first-person shooters like "Counter-Strike" and battle royales like "Fortnite."

The inclusive nature of eSports has made it accessible to a broad audience. Online platforms allow anyone with an internet connection to participate, whether by playing, streaming, or simply watching. This inclusivity has been a driving force behind the rapid growth of eSports fandom.

Community and Identity

For many fans, eSports is more than just entertainment; it is a significant part of their identity. Being an eSports fan involves being part of a community that shares a common passion. Fans often form strong bonds with each other through online interactions, fan clubs, and local meetups.

These communities provide a sense of belonging and purpose. Fans take pride in supporting their favorite teams and players, often participating in fan art, fan fiction, and other creative expressions of their fandom. The sense of community and identity is further reinforced by the shared experiences of watching live streams, attending events, and discussing the latest developments in the eSports world.

The Economic Impact of Fandom

The rise of eSports fandom has had a significant economic impact on the industry. Fans drive demand for merchandise, tickets to live events, and premium content subscriptions. Sponsorship deals and advertising revenue are also heavily influenced by the size and engagement of the fan base.

As eSports continues to grow, the economic influence of its fans will only increase. Companies are investing more in eSports marketing, recognizing the value of reaching this dedicated and engaged audience. This investment, in turn, fuels further growth and development within the industry, creating a positive feedback loop.

The rise of eSports fandom is a testament to the power of community and shared passion. From the early days of local gatherings to the global phenomenon it is today, eSports fandom has played a crucial role in shaping the industry. As the eSports community continues to grow and evolve, its influence will undoubtedly continue to drive the industry forward.

eSports and Mainstream Media

eSports has experienced a significant transformation from a niche pastime to a mainstream entertainment phenomenon. A crucial part of this transition has been its relationship with mainstream media. The integration of eSports into traditional media channels has not only elevated its visibility but has also provided new opportunities for growth and engagement.

Initial Media Skepticism

Initially, mainstream media outlets were skeptical of eSports, viewing it as a niche interest with limited appeal. Early coverage was sporadic and often lacked depth, reflecting a broader uncertainty about the legitimacy and potential of competitive gaming. However, as eSports began to attract larger audiences and generate significant revenue, media perceptions started to shift.

The Turning Point: High-Profile Partnerships

The turning point came when major media companies recognized the potential of eSports to attract young, tech-savvy audiences. Partnerships with established sports networks like ESPN, Fox Sports, and the BBC marked a significant milestone. These networks began broadcasting major eSports tournaments, giving them the same treatment as traditional sports events. This move not only legitimized eSports but also introduced it to a wider audience.

The Role of Streaming Platforms

Streaming platforms like Twitch and YouTube Gaming played a pivotal role in bridging the gap between eSports and mainstream media. These platforms provided a space where eSports content could thrive and reach millions of viewers worldwide. The success of streaming platforms demonstrated the massive demand for eSports content, which in turn attracted the attention of traditional media.

Integrating eSports into Traditional Sports Networks

Sports networks started integrating eSports into their regular programming. Major tournaments like the League of Legends World Championship, The International (Dota 2), and the Overwatch League found their way onto traditional television broadcasts. These events were covered with the same rigor and enthusiasm as other major sports events, complete with professional commentary, analysis, and high production values.

This integration helped in normalizing eSports as a legitimate form of competition and entertainment. Viewers who might not have been exposed to eSports otherwise were introduced to the excitement and skill involved in competitive gaming. This broader exposure helped grow the eSports fanbase and brought in new demographics.

Documentary Films and Series

Documentary films and series have also played a significant role in bringing eSports to mainstream audiences. Productions like "Free to Play," "All Work All Play," and "7 Days Out" provided in-depth looks at the lives of professional gamers and the inner workings of eSports tournaments. These documentaries humanized the players, showcasing their dedication, challenges, and triumphs. They helped break down stereotypes about gaming and highlighted the parallels between eSports athletes and traditional sports professionals.

Coverage in Print and Online Media

Print and online media have followed suit, with major publications like The New York Times, Forbes, and The Guardian regularly covering eSports events, industry trends, and player profiles. This coverage has further legitimized eSports and provided insightful analysis and commentary, helping to educate the public about the complexities and business aspects of the industry.

The Influence of Social Media

Social media has amplified the reach of eSports and its integration into mainstream media. Platforms like X, Instagram, and Facebook are used extensively by eSports organizations, players, and fans to share content, engage with audiences, and promote events. Social media campaigns and viral content have significantly boosted the visibility of eSports, making it an integral part of popular culture.

The Economic Impact

The integration of eSports into mainstream media has had a substantial economic impact. Advertising revenues have surged as brands seek to reach the engaged eSports audience. Sponsorship deals and media rights agreements have become more lucrative, reflecting the growing value of eSports as a media property. This influx of investment has fueled further growth and innovation within the industry.

Future Prospects

The relationship between eSports and mainstream media is poised for further growth. As media companies continue to explore new ways to engage audiences, eSports will play a crucial role. Innovations in broadcasting, such as virtual reality and interactive content, could further enhance the viewing experience and attract new fans. Additionally, the ongoing collaboration between traditional sports entities and eSports organizations will likely lead to more cross-promotion and integrated entertainment experiences.

eSports' journey into mainstream media has been transformative, broadening its reach and solidifying its status as a major entertainment force. The synergy between eSports and traditional media continues to evolve, promising exciting developments and opportunities for both industries.

Global Impact and Diversity

The global impact and diversity of eSports are among its most defining and exciting characteristics. What began as a series of localized gaming competitions has evolved into a worldwide phenomenon, bringing together players and fans from every corner of the globe. This section explores how eSports has transcended cultural and geographical boundaries, fostering a diverse and inclusive community while having a significant impact on various aspects of society.

The Worldwide Appeal of eSports

eSports has a unique ability to connect people across different cultures and languages. Games like "League of Legends," "Dota

2," and "Counter-Strike: Global Offensive" have massive followings in regions as diverse as North America, Europe, Asia, and Latin America. This global appeal is partly due to the universal nature of gaming, where the only requirement is an internet connection and a passion for the game.

Major eSports tournaments often feature teams from around the world, showcasing a variety of playing styles and strategies. Events like the League of Legends World Championship and The International are watched by millions globally, with live streams available in multiple languages. These tournaments not only highlight the skill of the players but also celebrate the rich cultural diversity of the eSports community.

Cultural Integration and Exchange

eSports has facilitated cultural exchange in ways that few other mediums can. International tournaments bring together players and fans from different backgrounds, promoting understanding and appreciation of different cultures. This cultural integration is evident in the way teams and players often incorporate elements of their heritage into their branding, celebrations, and interactions with fans.

For example, South Korea is renowned for its dominance in games like "StarCraft" and "League of Legends." The country's gaming culture, characterized by rigorous training regimens and professional infrastructure, has become a model for other regions. Meanwhile, Western teams have brought their own flair and innovation, creating a dynamic interplay of styles and strategies.

The global nature of eSports also means that fans are exposed to a wide range of cultural influences. Watching a match between a European and an Asian team, for instance, can be an enlightening experience that goes beyond the game itself, offering insights into different cultural attitudes towards competition, teamwork, and resilience.

Inclusivity and Representation

One of the most empowering aspects of eSports is its inclusivity. Unlike many traditional sports, eSports provides a level playing field where physical attributes are less important than skill, strategy, and dedication. This has opened up competitive gaming to a more diverse range of participants, including those who might not have the opportunity to excel in physical sports.

eSports has seen significant progress in terms of gender diversity, although challenges remain. Women and non-binary players are increasingly finding their place in the competitive scene, with initiatives aimed at promoting inclusivity and reducing harassment. Tournaments dedicated to women, like the GirlGamer Festival, highlight the talent and potential of female gamers and help break down barriers.

Furthermore, eSports transcends socioeconomic boundaries. The relatively low cost of entry, especially compared to traditional sports, means that talented players from less affluent backgrounds can compete on an equal footing with those from wealthier regions. This democratization of competitive gaming is fostering a more diverse and inclusive community.

Educational and Economic Impact

The impact of eSports extends beyond entertainment, influencing education and the economy. Educational institutions around the world are recognizing the value of eSports, with many offering scholarships and building programs to support aspiring professional gamers. These initiatives not only provide opportunities for players but also emphasize the development of valuable skills such as teamwork, strategic thinking, and time management.

Economically, eSports is a rapidly growing industry that generates significant revenue and creates jobs. From event organizers and broadcasters to marketers and game developers, a wide range of professionals are finding opportunities in this vibrant sector. Cities that host major tournaments also benefit from increased tourism and economic activity, underscoring the broader impact of eSports on local economies.

The Role of Technology

Technological advancements have played a crucial role in enabling the global reach and diversity of eSports. High-speed internet, streaming platforms, and social media have made it possible for anyone, anywhere, to participate in and enjoy eSports. These technologies have also facilitated the formation of online communities where fans can connect, share experiences, and support their favorite players and teams.

Virtual reality and augmented reality are emerging technologies that promise to further enhance the eSports experience. These innovations can create more immersive viewing experiences and provide new ways for fans to engage with the games and each other, potentially expanding the global reach of eSports even further.

The global impact and diversity of eSports are central to its identity and success. By bridging cultural divides and promoting inclusivity, eSports is not only redefining entertainment but also contributing to a more connected and understanding world. As the industry continues to grow and evolve, its ability to unite people from diverse backgrounds will remain one of its greatest strengths.

Chapter 6: Legal and Ethical Landscape

Regulation and Governance

As eSports has grown into a global industry, the need for regulation and governance has become increasingly apparent. Effective regulation ensures fair play, protects the rights of players, and maintains the integrity of competitions. Governance structures also help to standardize practices across different regions and organizations, providing a coherent framework for the industry's continued growth.

Establishing Regulatory Bodies

The formation of regulatory bodies has been a crucial step in organizing the eSports industry. These organizations oversee the enforcement of rules and standards to ensure that competitions are fair and transparent. One of the most prominent regulatory bodies is the Esports Integrity Commission (ESIC), established to maintain integrity within the industry. ESIC addresses issues like match-fixing, doping, and other unethical practices, promoting a fair competitive environment.

In addition to ESIC, various national and international bodies have emerged to govern eSports in specific regions or games. For instance, the Korean e-Sports Association (KeSPA) plays a vital role in regulating eSports in South Korea, one of the industry's largest markets. These organizations work closely with game developers, tournament organizers, and teams to implement and enforce regulations.

Standardizing Player Contracts

Player contracts are a critical aspect of eSports governance. In the early days of competitive gaming, contracts were often informal and varied widely in terms of player rights and obligations. Today, standardizing these contracts is essential to protect players and ensure fair treatment.

Regulatory bodies and associations have developed guidelines for player contracts, covering aspects such as salary, benefits, playing time, and conditions for termination. These standardized contracts help prevent exploitation and provide players with security and stability in their careers. They also outline ethical guidelines and responsibilities, ensuring that players uphold the standards expected in professional competition.

Addressing Doping and Fair Play

Doping is a concern in any competitive sport, and eSports is no exception. The use of performance-enhancing drugs (PEDs) can give players an unfair advantage, undermining the integrity of competitions. Regulatory bodies like ESIC and individual game publishers have implemented strict anti-doping policies to address this issue.

Regular drug testing is conducted at major tournaments to ensure compliance with these policies. Education programs are also in place to inform players about the risks and consequences of using PEDs. By maintaining rigorous anti-doping measures, the industry can ensure that victories are achieved through skill and effort alone.

Combatting Match-Fixing and Betting Scandals

Match-fixing and betting scandals have occasionally plagued eSports, threatening its integrity and reputation. These activities not only harm the competitive spirit but also damage the trust of fans and stakeholders. Regulatory bodies are tasked with investigating and preventing such activities to maintain the credibility of the sport.

Advanced monitoring systems are used to detect unusual betting patterns and potential match-fixing. Offenders face severe penalties, including fines, suspensions, and lifetime bans. These measures are essential for preserving the integrity of eSports and ensuring that competitions are decided by fair play.

Ensuring Inclusivity and Diversity

Governance in eSports also involves promoting inclusivity and diversity. Historically, the industry has faced challenges regarding gender representation and diversity among players and audiences. Regulatory bodies and organizations are working to create a more inclusive environment.

Initiatives include promoting female and minority participation, creating safe and welcoming spaces for all players, and implementing strict anti-harassment policies. These efforts aim to broaden the appeal of eSports and ensure that it reflects the diversity of the global gaming community.

Protecting Intellectual Property

Intellectual property (IP) rights are another crucial area of regulation in eSports. Game publishers hold the IP rights to the games used in competitions, and these rights must be respected by teams, players, and tournament organizers. Governance structures help manage the use of these IPs, ensuring that they are used legally and ethically.

Agreements between publishers and eSports organizations outline the terms of use for games in competitive settings. These agreements cover broadcasting rights, licensing fees, and other important aspects. Proper management of IP rights ensures that the creators of the games are fairly compensated and that their work is protected.

Promoting Global Standards

As eSports is a global industry, establishing consistent standards across different regions is essential. International regulatory bodies work to harmonize rules and practices, facilitating smoother operations for global tournaments and ensuring fair competition regardless of location.

Global standards cover various aspects of eSports, including player eligibility, tournament formats, and disciplinary procedures. By adopting these standards, the industry can ensure a level playing field for all participants, fostering a more cohesive and professional environment.

Regulation and governance are fundamental to the success and sustainability of eSports. Effective oversight ensures fair play, protects the rights of players, and maintains the integrity of competitions. As the industry continues to grow, robust regulatory frameworks will be crucial in navigating the challenges and opportunities that lie ahead.

Player Rights and Contracts

The rapid professionalization of eSports has brought significant attention to player rights and contracts. As eSports grows, ensuring fair treatment and clear agreements between players and organizations becomes increasingly crucial. This section delves into the various aspects of player rights, the structure of eSports contracts, and the evolving landscape of these agreements.

The Evolution of Player Contracts

In the early days of eSports, player contracts were often informal or non-existent. Players joined teams based on verbal agreements or simple written documents, with little legal oversight. As the industry matured, the need for more structured and legally binding contracts became apparent. Today, contracts are a standard practice, outlining the obligations and rights of both players and organizations.

A typical eSports contract covers various elements, including salary, performance expectations, sponsorship obligations, and termination conditions. These contracts ensure that players are compensated fairly and that teams can rely on their players to fulfill certain commitments.

Key Elements of eSports Contracts

1. **Salary and Compensation**: One of the most critical aspects of any contract is the player's salary. Contracts specify the amount a player will be paid, the payment schedule, and any bonuses or incentives based on performance. Compensation packages may also include benefits such as health insurance, housing allowances, and travel expenses.

2. **Performance Expectations**: Contracts often outline the performance standards expected from players. This can include participation in a set number of practice hours, maintaining a certain level of physical fitness, and

achieving performance metrics in competitions. These clauses ensure that players remain committed to their professional responsibilities.

3. **Sponsorship and Branding**: Players are often required to participate in promotional activities for team sponsors. Contracts detail these obligations, such as wearing sponsor-branded apparel, appearing in advertisements, and engaging with fans on social media. These activities help generate revenue for the team and enhance the player's marketability.

4. **Termination Clauses**: Contracts include terms under which either party can terminate the agreement. Common reasons for termination include breach of contract, poor performance, or personal misconduct. Clear termination clauses protect both the player and the organization, providing a legal framework for resolving disputes.

5. **Intellectual Property Rights**: Players' images, in-game personas, and personal brands are valuable assets. Contracts address the ownership and usage rights of these assets, ensuring that players retain control over their personal brand while allowing teams to use their likeness for promotional purposes.

Protecting Player Rights

As the industry grows, there has been increasing awareness of the need to protect player rights. Issues such as long working hours, lack of job security, and unfair compensation have come to the forefront. Several measures are being taken to address these concerns.

1. **Standardized Contracts**: Efforts are underway to develop standardized contracts that provide a baseline for fair treatment of players. These contracts ensure consistency in terms and conditions across the industry, protecting players from exploitative practices.

2. **Players' Associations**: Similar to traditional sports, players' associations are emerging in eSports. These organizations advocate for player rights, offer legal support, and work to improve working conditions. The establishment of the Esports Players League (ESPL) is one such example, providing a collective voice for players.

3. **Legal Recourse**: Players are becoming more aware of their legal rights and the importance of seeking legal advice before signing contracts. Legal professionals specializing in eSports law are helping players understand their contracts and ensuring their interests are protected.

4. **Mental and Physical Health**: Recognizing the intense demands of professional gaming, teams are investing in resources to support the mental and physical health of their players. This includes hiring psychologists, providing access to fitness facilities, and encouraging a healthy work-life balance.

Challenges and Future Directions

Despite progress, challenges remain in ensuring fair treatment for eSports players. The rapid pace of industry growth means that regulatory frameworks often lag behind. Issues such as international contracts, jurisdictional differences, and the enforcement of labor laws in a digital context require ongoing attention.

Looking forward, the eSports industry is likely to see continued efforts to standardize contracts and enhance player protections. Collaboration between teams, players, legal experts, and industry bodies will be essential in creating an environment that supports the well-being and success of professional gamers.

The development of robust player rights and contracts is a vital component of the professional eSports ecosystem. As the industry matures, these frameworks will play a crucial role in ensuring fair treatment and fostering a sustainable, thriving eSports environment.

Ethical Issues in eSports

The rapid growth of eSports has brought with it a range of ethical issues that need to be addressed to ensure the industry's integrity and sustainability. These issues span player welfare, fair competition, and the responsibilities of organizations within the eSports ecosystem.

Player Exploitation and Welfare

One of the most pressing ethical concerns in eSports is the potential exploitation of players. Many professional gamers are young, and some enter the competitive scene as teenagers. Without proper regulations, these young players can be vulnerable to exploitation through unfair contracts, inadequate compensation, and excessive training demands.

Ensuring player welfare involves implementing fair contracts that provide adequate salaries, health benefits, and reasonable working conditions. Organizations must also consider the physical and mental health of players. The intense nature of competitive gaming can lead to burnout, stress, and other health issues. Providing access to medical professionals, psychologists, and proper rest periods is essential for maintaining the well-being of players.

Cheating and Integrity

Cheating undermines the fundamental principles of fair competition in eSports. This includes using unauthorized software (hacks), exploiting in-game bugs, or any other actions that give an unfair advantage. Such practices not only distort competition results but also damage the credibility of eSports as a legitimate sport.

To combat cheating, strict anti-cheat measures and regular monitoring are necessary. Game developers and tournament organizers must work together to ensure robust anti-cheat systems are in place. When cheating is detected, appropriate disciplinary actions, including bans and fines, should be enforced to maintain the integrity of the sport.

Match-Fixing and Betting

Match-fixing, where players or teams deliberately lose games to benefit from betting, is another significant ethical issue. This practice compromises the integrity of competitions and erodes trust among fans and stakeholders. The growing popularity of eSports betting has increased the risk of match-fixing.

Addressing this issue requires collaboration between regulatory bodies, betting companies, and eSports organizations. Implementing stringent monitoring systems to detect irregular betting patterns and establishing clear consequences for those involved in match-fixing are crucial steps. Education programs for players about the risks and repercussions of match-fixing can also help prevent these unethical practices.

Doping and Performance Enhancing Drugs

The use of performance-enhancing drugs (PEDs) to gain an unfair advantage is a concern in eSports, just as it is in traditional sports. Stimulants that improve reaction times and concentration can provide players with an edge in competition. The ethical issue arises from the unfair advantage these substances offer and the potential health risks to players.

Anti-doping regulations, regular testing, and strict penalties for violations are necessary to combat this issue. Educating players about the dangers and ethical implications of PED use can also help maintain fair play. Creating a culture of clean competition is essential for the credibility and health of the eSports industry.

Representation and Inclusivity

eSports has faced criticism for a lack of diversity and inclusivity, particularly concerning gender representation. Female players and players from minority groups often encounter harassment, discrimination, and fewer opportunities. Addressing these ethical issues is vital for creating a more inclusive and equitable eSports environment.

Promoting diversity involves actively supporting and encouraging participation from underrepresented groups. Implementing strict anti-harassment policies, providing equal opportunities for all players, and celebrating diversity through inclusive marketing and representation can help create a welcoming environment. Organizations and communities must work together to foster a culture of respect and inclusion.

Streaming and Content Creation Ethics

With the rise of streaming and content creation, ethical concerns related to online behavior and content have emerged. Streamers and content creators have significant influence, and their actions and words can impact their audience. Ethical issues include promoting harmful behavior, misleading content, and inappropriate advertising.

Streamers and content creators should adhere to ethical guidelines that promote positive behavior and responsible content. Platforms like Twitch and YouTube have a role to play in enforcing these standards, ensuring that their communities remain safe and respectful. Transparency in advertising and sponsorships is also crucial to maintain trust with viewers.

Sponsorship and Commercial Influence

The influence of sponsors and commercial interests in eSports can lead to ethical dilemmas. While sponsorships provide essential funding, they can also create conflicts of interest and pressure to prioritize profit over the integrity of the sport. Ensuring that commercial relationships do not compromise competitive fairness or player welfare is vital.

Transparent and ethical sponsorship agreements that prioritize the interests of players and the integrity of competitions are necessary. Organizations must balance commercial interests with the core values of eSports, ensuring that their actions do not undermine the trust of fans and stakeholders.

Protecting Intellectual Property and Copyright

Intellectual property (IP) and copyright issues are significant in the digital world of eSports. This includes the use of game content, streaming rights, and the creation of derivative works. Respecting IP rights ensures that creators and developers are fairly compensated for their work.

Clear guidelines and agreements regarding the use of IP and copyrights in eSports can help navigate these ethical concerns. Collaboration between game developers, content creators, and legal experts is essential to ensure that IP rights are respected and protected.

The ethical issues in eSports are complex and multifaceted, requiring ongoing attention and proactive measures from all stakeholders. Addressing these challenges is crucial for the sustainability and credibility of the industry, ensuring that eSports can continue to grow as a respected and fair competitive sport.

Chapter 7: The Future of eSports

Trends Shaping the Future

The future of eSports is bright and dynamic, driven by several key trends that are poised to transform the industry. From technological advancements to evolving business models, these trends are shaping how eSports will develop in the coming years. This section explores the most significant trends that are influencing the future of competitive gaming.

Technological Innovations

Technology continues to be a major driver of change in eSports. One of the most exciting advancements is the integration of Virtual Reality and Augmented Reality into competitive gaming. VR and AR can create immersive gaming experiences that were previously unimaginable, providing players and spectators with a new level of engagement.

5G technology is another game-changer, offering faster and more reliable internet connections. This will enhance the quality of online gaming and live streaming, reducing latency and allowing for more complex and graphically intensive games to be played competitively. With 5G, mobile eSports are expected to grow, making competitive gaming more accessible to a broader audience.

Artificial Intelligence (AI) is also set to play a significant role. AI can be used to develop smarter non-player characters (NPCs), analyze player performance, and create personalized training programs. AI-driven analytics can help teams devise better strategies and give fans deeper insights into the games.

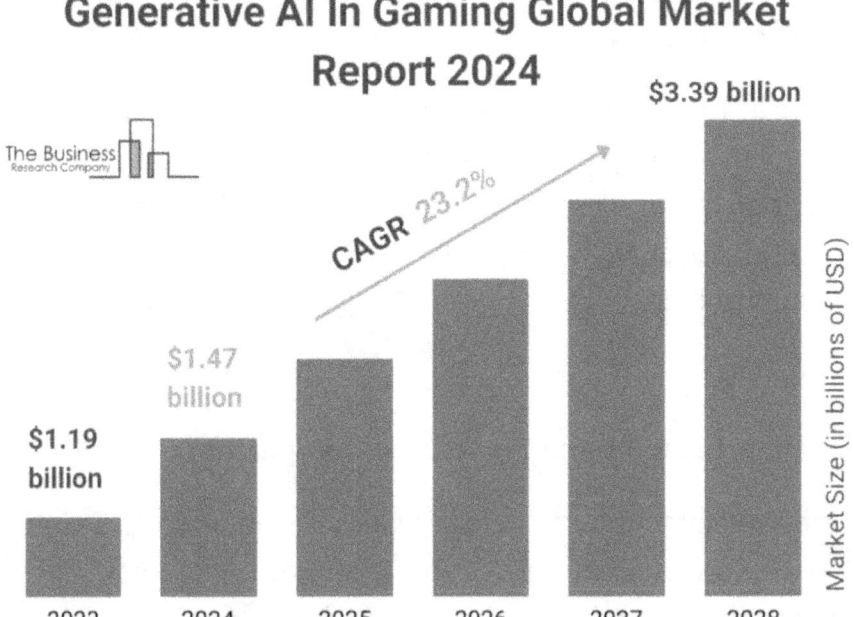

Growth of Mobile eSports

Mobile eSports is rapidly gaining traction, particularly in regions where smartphones are more accessible than gaming PCs or consoles. Games like "PUBG Mobile," "Free Fire," and "Arena of Valor" have huge player bases and competitive scenes. The convenience of mobile gaming allows players to compete from anywhere, making it easier to participate in and watch eSports events.

The rise of mobile eSports is also attracting significant investment from game developers, sponsors, and tournament organizers. As mobile hardware improves and games become more sophisticated, the quality and popularity of mobile eSports are likely to increase.

Franchise Leagues and Structured Competition

The establishment of franchise leagues, similar to traditional sports leagues, is becoming more common in eSports. These leagues offer stability for teams and players by providing consistent schedules, revenue sharing, and long-term planning.

The Overwatch League (OWL) and the Call of Duty League (CDL) are examples of successful franchise models.

Franchise leagues help professionalize the industry, attracting more significant investments from traditional sports team owners, media companies, and global brands. This structured approach also enhances fan engagement by creating clear narratives and rivalries, much like traditional sports.

Expansion of Media Rights and Broadcasting

As eSports continues to grow, media rights and broadcasting deals are becoming increasingly important. Streaming platforms like Twitch, YouTube Gaming, and Facebook Gaming have been central to eSports' rise, but traditional media companies are also starting to take notice. Networks like ESPN, TBS, and BBC have begun broadcasting eSports events, bringing competitive gaming to a broader audience.

These broadcasting deals are lucrative, providing essential revenue for teams and organizers. They also help legitimize eSports as a mainstream form of entertainment, attracting more viewers and sponsors.

Increased Focus on Player Well-being

The intense demands of professional gaming have brought player well-being to the forefront. Teams and organizations are investing more in the mental and physical health of their players. This includes hiring psychologists, providing fitness and nutritional support, and encouraging a balanced lifestyle.

This trend is crucial for the sustainability of the industry. Ensuring that players can maintain long and healthy careers benefits everyone involved, from the players themselves to the fans and the organizations that support them.

Diversification of Revenue Streams

Diversification of revenue streams is essential for the long-term viability of eSports. While sponsorships and advertising remain significant sources of income, other avenues are being explored. Merchandise sales, including team apparel and branded accessories, are becoming more popular.

Crowdfunding and fan support platforms like Patreon allow fans to directly support their favorite players and teams. Additionally, the use of blockchain technology and non-fungible tokens (NFTs) offers new ways to monetize digital assets and create unique fan experiences.

Globalization and Regional Growth

eSports is a global phenomenon, and its growth varies by region. Asia, particularly South Korea and China, remains a powerhouse in competitive gaming, but other regions are catching up. North America and Europe have well-established scenes, and emerging markets in Latin America, the Middle East, and Africa are showing significant potential.

Localized leagues and tournaments are helping to nurture talent and build fan bases in these regions. This regional growth is essential for the global expansion of eSports, ensuring that it remains diverse and inclusive.

Integration with Traditional Sports

The lines between eSports and traditional sports are increasingly blurring. Traditional sports teams are investing in eSports, creating their own teams and hosting tournaments. This integration brings mutual benefits, with traditional sports organizations gaining access to younger audiences and eSports gaining legitimacy and expertise from established sports entities.

Collaborations between eSports and traditional sports are also leading to innovative content and marketing strategies. For example, virtual versions of traditional sports games, like FIFA and NBA 2K, offer new ways for fans to engage with their favorite sports in a digital format.

These trends highlight the dynamic and rapidly evolving nature of the eSports industry. As technology advances and the industry matures, eSports will continue to grow and transform, offering exciting opportunities and experiences for players, fans, and stakeholders worldwide. The future of eSports is not only bright but also full of potential, as it continues to break new ground and reach unprecedented heights.

Potential Challenges

The eSports industry, despite its rapid growth and increasing popularity, faces several potential challenges that could impact its future development. These challenges span regulatory, economic, and social aspects, each requiring careful navigation to ensure the sustained success of the industry.

Regulatory Hurdles

As eSports continues to expand globally, differing regulations across countries pose significant challenges. Each region has its own set of rules regarding gambling, player contracts, and competition laws. Navigating this patchwork of regulations can be complex for international tournaments and organizations.

For example, some countries have strict laws against online gambling, which affects the betting markets associated with eSports. Additionally, labor laws vary widely, complicating the management of international teams and player contracts. Harmonizing these regulations or finding ways to comply with diverse legal frameworks is essential for the global growth of eSports.

Economic Viability

Ensuring economic sustainability remains a critical challenge. While the eSports market is growing, not all organizations and events are profitable. Many rely heavily on sponsorships and external funding, which can be unstable. The industry needs to develop more diverse and reliable revenue streams to ensure long-term viability.

Ticket sales, merchandising, and direct-to-consumer content are potential growth areas, but they require significant investment and strategic planning. Additionally, smaller organizations often struggle to compete financially with established teams, leading to a risk of market consolidation that could stifle diversity and innovation in the industry.

Player Welfare

Maintaining player welfare is another pressing issue. The intense competitive environment and the demands of constant training and competition can lead to physical and mental health problems. Burnout is a common issue among professional players, some of whom start their careers at a very young age.

Organizations need to prioritize the health and well-being of their players by providing adequate support, including mental health resources, physical training, and reasonable schedules. Ensuring a healthy work-life balance is crucial for sustaining the careers of eSports athletes and maintaining the industry's overall health.

Technological Dependence

eSports is inherently tied to technology, and this dependence can be a double-edged sword. While technological advancements drive the industry forward, they also introduce vulnerabilities. Issues such as server reliability, cybersecurity threats, and the rapid obsolescence of gaming hardware can pose significant risks.

Cybersecurity, in particular, is a growing concern. High-profile tournaments and players are attractive targets for cyber-attacks, which can disrupt events and compromise sensitive data. Investing in robust security measures and staying ahead of technological threats is essential for maintaining the integrity and safety of eSports competitions.

Market Saturation

The rapid growth of eSports has led to a crowded market with numerous games, leagues, and tournaments vying for attention. This saturation can dilute audience engagement and spread resources thinly across too many platforms. Not every game or tournament can achieve mainstream success, leading to potential financial losses and the collapse of lesser-known leagues.

To address this, the industry must focus on quality over quantity, supporting well-organized and popular games and events. Strategic partnerships and collaborations can help consolidate resources and audiences, ensuring that eSports maintains a strong and dedicated fanbase.

Public Perception and Legitimacy

Despite its growth, eSports still faces skepticism and misunderstanding from parts of the general public and media. Some view competitive gaming as less legitimate than traditional sports, which can affect its acceptance and support from broader audiences and potential sponsors.

Improving public perception involves educating audiences about the skills, dedication, and professionalism required in eSports. Highlighting the parallels with traditional sports, such as teamwork, strategy, and physical training, can help bridge the understanding gap. Positive media coverage and public endorsements from respected figures in traditional sports and entertainment can also enhance legitimacy.

Ethical and Social Issues

Ethical and social issues, including diversity, inclusivity, and harassment, continue to challenge the eSports community. The industry has faced criticism for its lack of diversity and instances of toxic behavior among players and fans. Addressing these issues is crucial for creating a welcoming and inclusive environment.

Promoting diversity involves active recruitment and support for underrepresented groups, including women and minorities. Implementing strict codes of conduct and anti-harassment policies, both online and at events, is essential for fostering a respectful and safe community. Organizations must take a proactive stance in addressing these issues to ensure the long-term health and inclusivity of eSports.

Environmental Impact

The environmental impact of eSports is an emerging concern. Large-scale events, extensive use of electronic equipment, and the energy consumption of streaming platforms contribute to the industry's carbon footprint. As global awareness of environmental issues grows, eSports organizations will need to adopt more sustainable practices.

This can include measures such as using energy-efficient technologies, implementing recycling programs at events, and offsetting carbon emissions. By taking steps to reduce their environmental impact, eSports organizations can contribute to global sustainability efforts and enhance their public image.

The eSports industry faces a range of potential challenges that require strategic planning and proactive management. Addressing regulatory complexities, ensuring economic sustainability, prioritizing player welfare, and tackling ethical issues are all crucial for the continued growth and success of eSports. By navigating these challenges effectively, the industry can build a resilient and thriving future.

Predictions and Opportunities

The eSports industry is poised for continued growth and transformation, presenting numerous opportunities for players, teams, investors, and fans. As we look ahead, several key trends and predictions can help us understand where eSports is heading and what opportunities lie ahead.

Mainstream Acceptance and Integration

eSports is on a trajectory to achieve broader mainstream acceptance. With increasing coverage from traditional media outlets and more partnerships with mainstream brands, eSports is becoming a regular part of the entertainment landscape. This integration will likely lead to more crossover events, where traditional sports and eSports come together, creating hybrid competitions and collaborative ventures.

This mainstream acceptance opens up opportunities for greater investment from non-endemic brands looking to tap into the youthful and tech-savvy eSports audience. Companies from various sectors, including automotive, fashion, and consumer electronics, are expected to increase their involvement, bringing in substantial sponsorship and advertising revenue.

Expansion of Educational Programs

Educational institutions are increasingly recognizing the value of eSports, not only as a competitive activity but also as a tool for learning and development. More schools and universities are expected to offer eSports scholarships, degrees, and training programs. These initiatives provide students with pathways to careers in game design, marketing, management, and broadcasting, beyond just playing professionally.

The expansion of educational programs presents opportunities for partnerships between educational institutions and eSports organizations. Such collaborations can foster the development of new talent, enhance the professionalism of the industry, and create a pipeline of skilled individuals ready to enter various roles within the eSports ecosystem.

Growth of Mobile eSports

Mobile gaming continues to surge in popularity, and mobile eSports is expected to follow suit. As smartphones become more powerful and mobile internet speeds increase with the rollout of 5G, mobile eSports will become more competitive and accessible. Games like "PUBG Mobile," "Call of Duty: Mobile," and "Clash Royale" are leading the charge, with more titles likely to emerge.

The growth of mobile eSports offers significant opportunities for game developers, hardware manufacturers, and telecom companies. Developers can create new titles optimized for competitive play, while hardware manufacturers can develop specialized gaming phones and accessories. Telecom companies can offer data packages and low-latency services tailored for gamers, capitalizing on this expanding market.

Enhanced Viewer Experience

The viewer experience in eSports will continue to evolve with advancements in technology. Virtual reality and augmented reality can create more immersive and interactive viewing experiences. Fans might soon be able to watch games from the perspective of their favorite players or interact with game elements in real-time.

Streaming platforms will also innovate, offering features like real-time statistics, multi-angle views, and interactive chat functions. These enhancements will make watching eSports more engaging and personalized, attracting a larger audience and increasing viewer retention.

These advancements provide opportunities for content creators, technology companies, and broadcasters to develop new products and services that enhance the spectator experience. Interactive and immersive technologies can set new standards for how eSports are consumed, making the experience more compelling for fans.

Esports Betting and Fantasy Leagues

Esports betting and fantasy leagues are poised for substantial growth. As regulations around gambling continue to evolve, more regions are expected to legalize and regulate eSports betting. This will lead to the development of sophisticated betting platforms and fantasy leagues, similar to those seen in traditional sports.

These developments present opportunities for companies to enter the eSports betting market, creating platforms that offer secure and engaging experiences for users. Additionally, fantasy leagues can drive fan engagement by allowing players to draft their dream teams and compete against others, further deepening their connection to the eSports they love.

Sustainable Business Models

As the eSports industry matures, there will be a greater focus on creating sustainable business models. Teams and organizations will look to diversify their revenue streams, moving beyond sponsorships and prize money. Merchandise sales, digital content, and subscription services will become increasingly important.

Opportunities abound for businesses to create products and services that cater to the needs of the eSports community. This includes everything from exclusive content and branded merchandise to training programs and lifestyle products. By diversifying their offerings, eSports organizations can build more stable and resilient businesses.

Inclusion and Diversity Initiatives

There will be continued efforts to promote inclusion and diversity within the eSports community. As awareness grows about the importance of representation, more initiatives will be launched to support underrepresented groups, including women and people from diverse ethnic backgrounds.

These initiatives create opportunities for organizations to lead in promoting diversity and inclusion. By fostering an inclusive environment, eSports can attract a broader range of talent and perspectives, enriching the industry and ensuring it reflects the diversity of its global audience.

International Expansion

The international expansion of eSports will continue, with emerging markets playing a crucial role. Regions like Southeast Asia, Latin America, and Africa are showing significant growth potential due to their young populations and increasing internet penetration.

Companies and organizations can capitalize on these emerging markets by establishing local leagues, investing in infrastructure, and creating content tailored to regional preferences. This global expansion will drive the next wave of growth for eSports, making it an even more diverse and widespread phenomenon.

The future of eSports is filled with exciting possibilities. As the industry evolves, new opportunities will emerge for players, teams, businesses, and fans. Those who can adapt to these changes and leverage the trends shaping the future will play a key role in the continued success and growth of eSports.

Conclusion

The world of eSports is a thrilling and rapidly evolving landscape, brimming with opportunities and challenges. From its humble beginnings to becoming a billion-dollar industry, eSports has captivated millions and reshaped the entertainment world. This book has explored the many facets of eSports, from the business strategies that drive it to the technological innovations that enhance it.

One of the most compelling aspects of eSports is its ability to bring people together from all corners of the globe. It transcends geographical, cultural, and language barriers, creating a universal platform where talent and passion can thrive. The community built around eSports is not just about the games but about the connections and shared experiences that make it vibrant and dynamic.

The business of eSports is multifaceted and complex, requiring a keen understanding of various revenue streams, from sponsorships to media rights and beyond. As the industry continues to grow, diversification and innovation in monetization strategies will be key to sustaining this growth. The insights shared by industry leaders highlight the importance of adaptability and foresight in navigating this ever-changing landscape.

Technological advancements continue to push the boundaries of what is possible in eSports. Virtual reality, augmented reality, and artificial intelligence are just a few of the innovations set to transform the experience for players and viewers alike. Embracing these technologies will open new dimensions of engagement and immersion, making the future of eSports even more exciting.

However, with growth comes responsibility. Ensuring the welfare of players, maintaining fair play, and fostering an inclusive environment are paramount. The industry's success will depend on how well it addresses these challenges, creating a sustainable and ethical ecosystem where everyone can thrive.

The future of eSports is bright, filled with endless possibilities. As we look ahead, it is clear that eSports will continue to play a significant role in the global entertainment landscape. Its ability to innovate, engage, and inspire sets it apart as one of the most dynamic industries today.

Thank you for embarking on this journey through the world of eSports. Whether you are a player, a fan, or a business professional, there is a place for you in this exciting field. The rise of gaming empires is just beginning, and you have the opportunity to be part of this incredible story.

Dear Reader,

I hope you found this book insightful and valuable.

Your feedback is invaluable to me. If you enjoyed this book, I would appreciate it if you could take a moment to leave a review on the reading apps and platforms.

Thank you for your support, and I wish you all the best.

Kind regards,
Ghazwan

About the Author

Ghazwan is a passionate entrepreneur and business strategist dedicated to helping individuals and organizations achieve their full potential with a deep understanding of modern businesses' challenges and opportunities.

With a Master's degree in Computer and Systems Sciences from Stockholm University, specializing in eService design, requirement engineering, and business process management, he is equipped to innovate cutting-edge solutions.

He believes in the power of collaboration and lifelong learning, and his mission is to empower people to reach their goals and positively impact the world.

www.ingramcontent.com/pod-product-compliance
Lightning Source LLC
Chambersburg PA
CBHW071929210526
45479CB00002B/607